Transformed by His Promises

TRANSFORMED
by
HIS PROMISES

A 12-Week Devotional
for Freedom from
the Psychological Slavery of
Life-Interfering Behaviors

*Renew Your Mind, Rewire Your Brain, and
Restore Your Life with Biblical Wisdom and Neuroscience*

KARL BENZIO , M.D.
ROSE ANN FORTE

Publishing support provided by
Ignite Press
55 Shaw Ave. #204
Clovis, CA 93612
www.IgnitePress.us

Cover design: Raffy Ferras Hoylar

ISBN: 979-8-9866084-6-4
ISBN: 979-8-9866084-7-1 Hardcover
ISBN: 979-8-9866084-8-8 Ebook

Praise for
Transformed by His Promises

"This twelve-week devotional will lead the reader through simple, yet effective, mental and spiritual exercises designed to develop godly habits for daily living that, over the course of 12 weeks, become wired into the brain and form a new foundation upon which to build, one victory after another until one becomes fully alive like Christ."

Timothy R. Jennings, M.D., DLFAPA
Medical Director, Honey Lake Clinic
President, Come and Reason Ministries
Author, *The God-Shaped Brain*

"The emphasis on Scripture, prayer, and gratitude make my recovery heart glad, while exercises in mindfulness, reflection and habit-change pack plenty of clinical punch. Grateful for the experience, vulnerability and hope these two partnering authors have brought to the table in order to give us something brand new, neuroscience with a heart!"

John Eklund, LCSW
Founder, Recovery Alive Inc.

"What I deeply appreciate about Dr. Karl Benzio and Rose Ann Forte is that God has positioned them as voices for integration, bringing together sound scientific research and the unshakable truth of God's Word."

Bob Hoskins
Founder, OneHope

"Transformed by His Promises is a practical and encouraging guide that blends biblical wisdom with science to help individuals overcome life-interfering behaviors. It offers powerful tools for lasting change, renewal, and freedom."

Greg Surratt
Founder, Pastors Collective

"As you read this devotional, you will find knowledge and freedom from the shackles that bind you. It will teach you the principles of the Word of God, and you will experience the free indeed life."

Anne Beiler
Founder, Auntie Anne's Pretzels
Author & Motivational Speaker

"Dr. Karl Benzio and Rose Ann Forte have created more than just a devotional; they've crafted a pathway to real change—one that's rooted in God's promises and backed by the way He designed our minds to work. This is a must-read for anyone looking to experience true renewal."

Rob Hoskins
President, OneHope

"Transformed by His Promises is a life-changing devotional that combines biblical wisdom with practical psychology, guiding readers to renew their minds and overcome destructive habits. It is a must-read for anyone seeking true transformation and healing."

Tim Timberlake
Senior Pastor, Celebration Church
Author

"Ever wondered how to actually change a behavior? Romans 12:1–3 speaks of renewing your mind, and psychology calls it neuroplasticity or rewiring your brain. This devotional breaks down these powerful concepts in an easy-to-understand, applicable way so you can experience real transformation."

John McGee
Founder, re|engage
Director, Watermark Resources

"Transformed by His Promises may be a 12-week devotional, but its impact will last a lifetime."

Rev. Ruth Hendrickson
Founder, RHM International & Mashah Ministry
Author, *Positioned: How to Be Aligned and Empowered to Walk into Your Divine Destiny*

"Transformed by His Promises is a life-giving guide that combines Scripture and brain science to renew your mind and rebuild your habits. If you're ready for real freedom in Christ and lasting change in life, this 12-week journey will show you the way."

Matthew Maher
Pastor, Landmark Church NJ

"For anyone struggling with life-interfering behaviors, this resource provides a scientifically grounded, spiritually rich path to lasting freedom."

Lisa Stewart
Chief Executive Officer, Honey Lake Clinic

"Reading these daily devotionals will better enable you to incorporate a biblical basis for the attributes of hope, gratitude, reflection, love, forgiving others and yourself, and making sound life choices. Many of the root issues and triggers for your dysfunctional behaviors will be revealed."

W. David Hager, M.D.
Physician, Author, Speaker

"Through Scripture, gratitude, and proven neuroscience, this devotional equips you to renew your mind, rewire your habits, and step into the freedom God has promised."

David E. Jenkins, Psy.D.
Professor & Clinical Director, Psy.D. in Clinical Psychology
Liberty University

"I was thrilled to review the devotional's insightful Scriptures and timeless truths which guide readers through a process of recovery and healing by building habits that lead to sustained sobriety. I know you will find it as valuable as I did."

Kurt R. Bravata, M.D., FASAM
Family & Addiction Medicine Physician
Member, American Society of Addiction Medicine

CONTENTS

Foreword

*A*s a physician, psychiatrist, and researcher, I have spent the better part of my professional life exploring the connections between faith, health, and well-being. Through decades of clinical work, scientific inquiry, and personal reflection, I have come to a deep conviction—one that is repeatedly affirmed in both the laboratory and the lives of those I have had the privilege to care for: Faith and science are not opposing forces. Rather, they are partners on a journey toward healing, renewal, growth, and flourishing.

It is with this conviction in mind that I commend to you the pages of this unique and timely 12-week devotional. It stands as a testament to the beautiful integration of spiritual wisdom, sound psychological principles, and cutting-edge scientific discoveries on neuroplasticity—the brain's remarkable capacity to change and heal itself over time. This is a work that not only speaks to the mind but also ministers to the heart and soul.

Many of us approach devotionals seeking comfort, guidance, or inspiration. Yet, this book offers something even deeper: an opportunity for genuine transformation. Its daily readings invite you to engage with Scripture not as distant words on ancient pages, but as living, breathing truth capable of rewiring your thoughts, renewing your emotional health, and reshaping the very architecture of your brain.

In my work at Duke University and beyond, I've observed countless individuals burdened by stress, depression, anxiety, and the wounds of past trauma. These conditions often lead to feelings of helplessness and despair. Yet, the message of both modern neuroscience and timeless Scripture is clear: Not just change, but full-life transformation is possible. Complete healing is a real possibility through an intimate connection with God. And God's design for the human brain, the ability to physically change through that connection with Him, includes a resilience and adaptability that we are only beginning to comprehend.

The scientific term *neuroplasticity* may sound complex, but it refers to a simple and profound truth: Our brains are not static. They are continually being molded and shaped by our experiences, thoughts, emotions, and behaviors. This means that the negative thought patterns and destructive habits that have held us captive for years can, by God's grace and with intentional practice, be transformed into patterns of hope, peace, and purpose.

The Apostle Paul spoke of this long before neuroscientists had the tools to observe it under a microscope. In his letter to the Romans, he exhorted believers, "Do not be conformed to this world, but be transformed by the renewing of your mind" (Romans 12:2, NIV). What Paul describes here is precisely what this devotional seeks to facilitate: a process of renewal that begins in the mind, flows into the heart, and manifests in a life that reflects God's redemptive power.

What makes this devotional distinctive—and why I am so pleased to introduce it—is its thoughtful integration of three domains often kept separate: Biblical truth, psychological skill-building, and the latest insights from brain science. Each daily entry presents Scripture not merely for reflection but for *application*, paired with practical exercises designed to activate neuroplastic change. You will be encouraged to meditate, to practice gratitude, to reframe negative thoughts, and to cultivate habits that enhance mental, emotional, and spiritual well-being.

These practices are not theoretical. They are grounded in decades of empirical research demonstrating how intentional actions can strengthen neural pathways associated with positive emotion, resilience, and faith. Scientific studies show that regular engagement in practices like prayer, meditation on Scripture, and expressions of gratitude can lead to measurable changes in brain structure and function. Regions of the brain associated with empathy, compassion, and self-regulation grow stronger. Areas linked to fear, stress, and negative rumination can quiet down. What modern imaging studies reveal today, believers have understood by faith for millennia: God's Word is living and active, and it has the power to heal and transform (Hebrews 4:12).

Yet this transformation is not automatic. As a clinician, I often remind patients that transformation requires both divine grace and Holy Spirit-powered human effort. God invites us into a partnership in which we actively participate in our healing. We make decisions each day—decisions about what we think about, how we respond to challenges, and where we place our focus. These decisions, repeated over time, lay down pathways in the brain that become roads well-traveled. This devotional guides you gently but persistently down those roads, showing you how to shift from patterns of fear and anxiety to patterns of faith and trust.

The book's structure—12 weeks of daily devotionals—reflects an understanding of how habits are formed and maintained. Research suggests it takes consistent repetition over several weeks to create lasting change in brain wiring. By engaging with these readings daily, you are not only learning; you are *training*. Just as physical exercise strengthens muscles over time, these spiritual and psychological exercises strengthen the mind and the spirit.

But what truly sets this work apart is its foundation in Christian faith. This is not a secular self-help manual dressed in religious language. It is deeply rooted in the life-giving truth of the Gospel. Its goal is not merely mental health, though that is a worthy aim; its goal is a deeper intimacy with the One who created you, redeems you, and calls you into fullness of life.

As a psychiatrist who has worked at the intersection of medicine and ministry, I have witnessed the power of faith to bring healing where medicine alone has fallen short. I have seen patients with chronic depression find hope through prayer and Scripture. I have watched individuals with anxiety disorders learn to experience peace through practices of mindfulness rooted in Christian meditation. I have had a front seat witnessing those imprisoned to life-interfering behaviors be set free as they apply the power of the Cross to their mind and lenses. I have been humbled to see how the truths of God's Word, applied faithfully, can do what no pill or therapy session can fully accomplish.

This book draws on those same truths. It invites you to step into a process of renewal that engages your whole being—body, mind, and spirit. It recognizes the complex interplay of brain chemistry, thought life, spiritual practice, and relationship with God. And it offers you a path forward that is both scientifically sound and spiritually rich.

You may be picking up this devotional because you are seeking relief from stress, healing from past wounds, guidance to stop life-interfering behaviors, or strength to face the future with courage. You may be a caregiver, a counselor, a pastor, or a friend, hoping to find tools that will help you walk alongside others in their journey. Wherever you are, and whatever has brought you to these pages, know this: You are not alone. God has not left you without resources. The Creator who formed your inmost being (Psalm 139:13) also designed your brain with the capacity to heal, to change, and to grow.

And He has given us, in His Word and in the gift of scientific insight, tools to participate in that healing. This book is one such tool. It is an invitation to trust not only in the wisdom of Scripture but in the goodness of the God who inspired it. It encourages you to embrace the disciplines that cultivate resilience and peace, and a reminder that you are being transformed, day by day, into the likeness of Christ (2 Corinthians 3:18).

As you journey through these 12 weeks, I pray you will discover not only new ways of thinking but new ways of being. May your heart be strengthened, your mind renewed, and your spirit lifted. And may the God of hope fill you with all joy and peace as you trust in Him (Romans 15:13).

Be BLESSED as you read this life-transforming devotional,

Harold G. Koenig, M.D., M.H.Sc.
Professor of Psychiatry & Behavioral Sciences
Associate Professor of Medicine
Director, Center for Spirituality, Theology, and Health
Duke University Medical Center, Durham, North Carolina

Preface

Why This Devotional Was Born

*M*y story started with a very serious alcohol problem that I couldn't find a solution for in any faith-based program I was aware of.

I was an entrepreneur with experience in high-level executive leadership. I also loved Jesus and served as a leader in church ministry. Because of the stigma I felt about my problem, I went outside of the church to find healing with a program that challenged me to put alcohol to the side for just 90 days. It was designed for entrepreneurs to help them switch their narrative around what it meant to go without drinking "attractively packaged poison" (as the founder of that organization liked to call it). I entered the coaching program without any intention of quitting forever. However, I was so transformed by all that happened inside those 90 days that I was hooked!

I ended up working with them as an Enrollment and Client Journey Coach and started learning more about the science behind changing mindsets and neural pathways. I realized that nearly everything they were teaching in that program was founded in biblical wisdom! In other words, they were teaching the Kingdom without the King! I felt prompted by the Holy Spirit to document what I learned in a daily devotional called *The Plans He Has For Me*. What began as a documentation of my journey in understanding the science behind renewing my mind (Romans 12:2) soon led to an international best-selling book, seven book awards, and powerful endorsements from leaders in faith and science.

Sometime after publishing the first edition of this devotional, I found myself seated in the audience at the American Association of Christian Counselors annual conference, listening to the Medical Director of that organization, Karl Benzio, M.D., explain the neuroscience of decision-making. I was so encouraged and excited after hearing him speak that I ran to the front of the room to tell him about this daily devotional I had developed for alcohol that followed the exact patterns and systems he had described in his talk.

We continued our discussions after the conference, and he realized how aligned we were in our thinking about how to heal from addiction. Dr. Karl ultimately recognized what I had long sensed in my spirit: These Kingdom-rooted, brain-informed truths aren't limited to alcohol or substances but speak to every *life-interfering behavior* that steals our joy and freedom. While I intuitively understood this broader application, it was Dr. Karl's collaborative voice, grounded in Practical NeuroTheology and clinical insight, that made the expansion into this new work possible.

Together, Dr. Karl and I have taken the core of *The Plans He Has For Me* and woven it into these pages, so that the same principles that transformed my own story can guide you toward the abundant life God promises, no matter which patterns you're ready to leave behind.

Blessings to you as you venture into this challenge to put a life-interfering behavior to the side for 84 consecutive days to understand the power of being transformed by His promises.

Rose Ann Forte

Introduction

Romans 7:18b-19 (ESV)

"For I have the desire to do what is right, but not the ability to carry it out. For I do not do the good I want, but the evil I do not want is what I keep on doing."

The apostle Paul's groan perfectly expressed how I felt in my late teens and early 20s..

In fact, I call it the Addict's Groan. Now, I don't think Paul was addicted to a substance, but rather to a pattern of life-interfering decisions and behaviors that stole some of his joy. As for me, I was addicted to alcohol, life-interfering behaviors, and dysfunctional patterns of thinking. Sure, I tried to stop, but… blah blah blah, then a bunch of lame excuses and finger pointing.

Eventually, after a DUI, I landed in jail for six felony counts of aggravated assault. Ugh! My rock bottom. But that's when God shared the plan He had for me, "Karl, you made me your Savior when you were a little kid, but you never made me the Lord of your life. If you make me the Lord of your life, I will renew your mind and transform your life, and then help you transform other people's lives as well."

> "For I know the plans I have for you," declares the Lord, "plans to prosper you and not to harm you, plans to give you hope and a future." Jeremiah 29:11 (NIV)

I was all in for sure! But how? What next?

You see, ever since I was five, God's call on my life was to integrate psychiatric science and biblical principles to understand decision-making skills. As the Ultimate Designer of everything, psychiatric science is just understanding how God designed our mind to work. The Bible is God's instruction manual for how to use our mind for abundance and flourishing living: B.I.B.L.E. — the Best Instruction Book for Living Everyday! I finally realized this integration would literally and figuratively be my "Get Out of Jail Free" card! That is, not just legal jail, but more importantly, the psychological prison in which my anxiety, insecurity, fear, anger, pride, impulsivity, and need for comfort had locked me up.

My healing journey took a couple of years, but over the last three decades, God's blessed me with a front row seat, helping so many patients start and navigate their healing journey. One of my passions is teaching my specialty, decision-making sciences, to equip both therapists and lay people to guide others in how to "reject man's wisdom by taking control of every thought (not just our conscious but especially our unconscious thoughts) to be aligned with Jesus so we can be consistent godly decision-makers" 2 Corinthians 10:4-6 (Dr Karl's paraphrasing). This Bible-Science integration I call Practical NeuroTheology.

Fast forward to a couple of years ago, I just finished presenting a workshop, weaving my transformation story and decision-making curriculum, at a huge world conference for 7,000 therapists and ministry workers. As I'm packing up my computer and fielding a long line of individual questions or comments, this random, wide-eyed and incredibly excited lady, after patiently waiting her turn, shares with me "Oh my gosh, your Practical NeuroTheology approach is exactly how God freed me from alcohol, and I've written a devotional for alcohol that is congruent with all of your teachings!"

I was on a high from presenting my favorite topic, and also in a rush to get to my next workshop. Being one of a rare species, a Christian psychiatrist, I am often approached with excitement about many of the concepts I teach. So, my first reaction to this stranger was skepticism. After exchanging contact info and receiving a copy of her devotional, Rose Ann called me a few weeks later. After sharing her transformation story through seamless blending of psychology and the Bible, with the caring and gentle nature she wrote, I realized how aligned we are. I congratulated her on her work and told her that I thought her work applied not only to alcohol and other substances, but also to all "life-interfering behaviors." Although she recognized the possibility of this being true, she asked me if I was willing to collaborate with her on an updated version of the devotional to reflect these ideas. I agreed, and this devotional reflects that collaboration.

This devotional combines our learned experiences and professional expertise that's empowered countless others through two key realizations. First, realizing our sin slate is washed perfectly clean. Jesus paid the ultimate cost, so we do not have to. If God doesn't hold your sins against you, can you do that for yourselves too? The second, realizing no one's memory banks are washed clean, so we show you how to take your conscious and unconscious thoughts captive, examining them in order to purge Satan's lies and distortions.

Can you imagine living your life moving forward with a clean sin slate? Then, learning how to clean your memory banks — how would that affect your thinking, your decisions, your behaviors? What if you could destroy shame, guilt, and strongholds that sabotage and derail your healing journey? How would that give you hope for living differently than you are now? How might it define and shape your future? Would it provide a vehicle for witnessing to others and being His light to show them the healing path?

Putting into practice these two realizations is a game changer, and the answers to the questions above change profoundly. Guilt and shame about our past transgressions are dream killers, and it is in this simple practice of knowing our sin slate is clean while cleaning up our memory banks that ultimately defeats the enemy who is doing everything in his power to separate us from God and pull us into the darkness and shadows where he operates.

This twelve-week journey was designed to reveal to you the power of the Holy Spirit and the truth of God's Word in action. As you focus each day on Scripture, you are given spiritual wisdom, psychological insight, and the practical tools to renew your mind — one decision at a time.

No matter what habit, mindset, or stronghold you came to confront and defeat, this devotional will serve as a roadmap so you will truly know: you are not a victim to your past! God has given each of us the mind of Christ and the power to choose, so we can form new empowering circuits and habits to not just replace the bad habit ones, but to actually renew and rewire our whole mind.

Thank you for inviting us into your inner space to help your healing journey. We pray this journey gives you the confidence, clarity, and courage to live out God's best in every area of your life and achieve your God-given potential and calling.

I love Jesus, and I hate when Satan wins any battle, so let's go!

by HIS grace,
Dr. Karl
Co-Founder and Chief Psychiatric Officer – Honey Lake Clinic
Medical Director – American Association of Christian Counselors

How to Use this Devotional

*T*his devotional is designed to be incorporated into a daily morning routine so new patterns of behavior and habits can be formed in place of old ones that have caused us much pain and consumed far more of our conscious thoughts than we would like to acknowledge. You are about to free up an enormous amount of time in your life by taking away one or more life-interfering behaviors. You will free up the time spent engaging in the behavior, unproductive time, and the time you spent negotiating with yourself about how you were going to manage this problem.

Your morning routine should include the following:

1. Start each day with the Lord's Prayer (Matthew 6:9-13). Below is the New Living Translation version. Feel free to use any version you feel comfortable with. Recite each line with acknowledgment and purpose. It is an all-encompassing prayer that incorporates everything you need to walk through each day. It acknowledges Him as our loving Father in Heaven, and that we must give Him the reverence He deserves. It acknowledges that He knows the end game. It acknowledges how He provides what we need each day and reminds us to confess our sins, seek forgiveness, and forgive the sins of others. Finally, it addresses the temptations we can anticipate each day, not only during these twelve weeks, but forevermore on this earth. Jesus told us to pray this way:

    > Our Father in heaven, may your name be kept holy.
    > May your Kingdom come soon.
    > May your will be done on earth, as it is in heaven.
    > Give us today the food we need, and forgive us our sins,
    > as we have forgiven those who sin against us.
    > And don't let us yield to temptation but rescue us from the evil one.

2. Get in the habit of daily gratitude. Write down *ten* things each day for which you are grateful. This will engage something called the reticular activating

system of your brain. It is a network of neurons that reminds us of what is important to us so it can filter out unnecessary information. To the extent we can fill this portion of our brain with thankfulness and gratitude, we will begin to look for evidence of it in our lives despite the enemy's efforts to have us focus and act out on the negative. Gratitude is what will provide us with joy despite circumstances. It doesn't have to be earth-shattering stuff. It can be something as simple as the appreciation of your morning coffee and your slippers, or something as humble as acknowledging you have eyes to see and ears to hear. Practice this daily, and you'll experience the transformational aspects of renewing your mind.

3. Read the daily Scripture and mindful minute, then take time to reflect and meditate on it. Write down your reflections and record your experiences, both positive and negative, throughout your journey. These reflections will play an important role in your choices to move forward after your twelve-week period.

4. Most importantly, *pray* each day. There is a prayer at the end of each day directly applicable to the verse, although you should feel free to pray whatever is in your heart. There's space at the end of each daily devotional for you to jot down your thoughts and additional prayer requests. If the space provided is not enough, feel free to keep a separate journal for writing down your reflections. Journaling is an important part of this journey.

Week 1: Days 1–7

Day 1

1 Timothy 4:15 (ESV)

Practice these things, immerse yourself in them, so that all may see your progress.

Mindful Minute

This journey is a journey of practice and rewiring the beautiful mind God created for each of us (or for *renewing* it as Paul writes in Romans 12).

He created a mind that saves us energy and remembers routine behaviors so we don't need to reteach them to ourselves each time we do them. Think about how we can drive to and from work and not remember how we even got there and back to our driveway. Think about the routine you do before you go to bed at night. There isn't much thought put into these things because it's the perfect energy-saving mechanism designed by our Creator.

When we allow sinful practices to enter our daily routines, those perfect energy-saving pathways are also engaged, except this time, the consequences can be harmful instead of helpful. During this twelve-week journey, we will commit to practicing a different way of processing our triggers related to any habit or behavior that interferes with living our best life. Twelve weeks is the target, so you may truly see your progress.

You can choose whatever path you believe is best for you after this period, but for these twelve weeks, we will start practicing our new habits and behaviors for the purpose of seeing progress and feeling how the Holy Spirit will work within you as you move away from destructive behaviors and toward healthy and godly ones.

Prayer

I am committed to practicing, Father. Let your Holy Spirit guide me as I embody integrity with my word to you during these twelve weeks. I will spend this period focused on your grace, love, and forgiveness. With your help, I will commit to living a life of appreciation for everything good in my life and give thanks to you. Lead me to walk steadily in the path of your Word for these twelve weeks so that my progress may be evident to me and to all I encounter. In Jesus' mighty name. Amen.

Daily Gratitude:

_____

_____

_____

_____

_____

_____

Reflections:

_____

_____

_____

_____

_____

_____

_____

_____

_____

Day 2

Romans 12:2 (ESV)

Do not be conformed to this world, but be transformed by the renewal of your mind, that by testing you may discern what is the will of God, what is good and acceptable and perfect.

Mindful Minute

As we enter day two of this challenge and commitment, what awaits you moving forward is powerful.

Our unconscious habit loop was created by our Heavenly Father to make our lives easier. However, when we allow the repeated practice of sin, we also allow the habit loop to take control of our lives. In the Garden of Eden, God gave Adam and Eve wisdom and His loving instruction. He told them they had the freedom to choose anything *except* the fruit from the Tree of Knowledge of Good and Evil. God warned them of the harm they would suffer if they chose to eat of this tree; they would die. Adam and Eve started rationalizing reasons why it would be okay if they disobeyed.

Today, the reason we are focusing on this twelve-week challenge is because, much like Adam and Eve, we justified a choice in the past that conformed to this world and created new neural networks and patterns. As a result, a habit loop developed that takes away an enormous amount of time, energy, and focus as our conscious thinking conflicts with our unconscious operating system.

By allowing ourselves to redirect this life-interfering behavior to something new and good, we give ourselves the ultimate gift of freeing up that time in favor of discernment about what is good and acceptable moving forward.

Prayer

Father, I pray today for transformation in my thinking that will allow me to have a clearer focus on your Word and instruction. I desire my thoughts to be occupied by something other than this habit that consumes my time, energy, and focus. I need your strength, Father, because of the psychological slavery this habit has created. I lost the spiritual battle through my choices but look forward to the freedom that can only be created in you. In Jesus' name. Amen.

Daily Gratitude:

_____

_____

_____

_____

_____

_____

Reflections:

_____

_____

_____

_____

_____

_____

_____

_____

Day 3

Philippians 4:6

Don't worry about anything; instead, pray about everything. Tell God what you need, and thank him for all he has done.

Mindful Minute

Sometimes, we can miss God's specific instructions within verses. His Word is living and breathing, and with each reading, we can look for different ways to interpret it.

Today, we focus on *thanksgiving*. Much has been done in the world on the power of living a life of gratitude versus one of expectation. Many self-help remedies involve practices of gratitude. Not surprisingly, God is the one who first instructed us to be grateful thousands of years ago. Ezra 3:11 says, "With praise and thanks they sang this song to the Lord." Psalm 7:17 states, "I will thank the Lord because he is just; I will sing praise to the name of the Lord Most High." 1 Thessalonians 5:18 says, "Be thankful in all circumstances. This is God's will for you who belong to Christ Jesus."

We focus our gratitude on God because good things are from God, who is our Ultimate Provider. When we begin to understand that the world is inherently broken, we can be truly grateful for the good God has gifted us with.

When gratitude and thanksgiving for all that our Creator provides are a focus of our daily lives, we can create a narrative that looks for something good and offset the negative with gratefulness. It will help us to look forward to something better and shift our mindset to His truth.

Prayer

Thank you for your wisdom, Father. I know everything good in this world originated from you. I will commit to practicing gratitude each day. I trust in you, Father, to see the world differently despite my current circumstances. In Jesus' name. Amen.

Daily Gratitude:

_____

_____

_____

_____

_____

_____

Reflections:

_____

_____

_____

_____

_____

_____

_____

_____

Day 4

Romans 5:1-5

Therefore, since we have been made right in God's sight by faith, we have peace with God because of what Jesus Christ our Lord has done for us. Because of our faith, Christ has brought us into this place of undeserved privilege where we now stand, and we confidently and joyfully look forward to sharing God's glory. We can rejoice, too, when we run into problems and trials, for we know that they help us develop endurance. And endurance develops strength of character, and character strengthens our confident hope of salvation. And this hope will not lead to disappointment. For we know how dearly God loves us, because he has given us the Holy Spirit to fill our hearts with his love.

Mindful Minute

Because of the Holy Spirit, we can rejoice in hope. While hope may be present through His Word, it is not always a felt experience because of the shame of sin, especially with a habit that controls our lives. Letting go of life-interfering behaviors is hard work that requires intentional redirection toward something better.

At the start of this journey, there will be times when we feel the suffering as we let go of behaviors that once consumed us. How do we endure this suffering? We do it by continuing our practice of daily gratitude because every good thing comes from God (James 1:17), and because we trust the promise of reigning with Him (2 Timothy 2:12).

God has promised us something better. You are closer to the finish line than you realize. Walking this path will produce endurance. Endurance produces character, and character anchors our hope. Our hope in Christ is a continual source of strength. It is steady and perseveres. Hope becomes evident in our character as we persevere.

Prayer

Thank you, Jesus, for dying on the cross and giving me access to peace through my faith in you. I want to experience the peace you offer. I am committed to this twelve-week process because I have hope, and I want to get rid of all the shame. I am tired of living a life where the shame of a habit occupies more time in my thoughts than the hopes and dreams I can access through you. I want to experience your plans, to prosper and impact others through my journey. I want people to see the quality of my character through you. In Jesus' name. Amen.

Daily Gratitude:

_____

_____

_____

_____

_____

_____

Reflections:

_____

_____

_____

_____

_____

_____

_____

_____

_____

Day 5

Psalm 66:10-12 (ESV)

For you, O God, have tested us; you have tried us as silver is tried. You brought us into the net; you laid a crushing burden on our backs; you let men ride over our heads; we went through fire and through water; yet you have brought us out to a place of abundance.

Mindful Minute

God's Word is full of verses related to how God refines us.

This verse describes the concept of being *tried* as silver is tried. There are many stories about how the silversmith refines his silver. The key concept of the story is how the silversmith must hold the silver over the heat so the impurities are separated from it. He must watch over this process every moment to know exactly when to pull it out of the fire. If he keeps it in the fire too long, it will be destroyed. Not only this, but the silversmith knows the refining process is complete when he can see his reflection in the silver, just as God knows His refining work in us begins to reflect His image.

These metaphors are perfect for our journey. This initial period of relinquishing our life-interfering habit may feel as if we are being given a crushing burden; however, we must know and trust that we are being refined through this process just long enough to remove the impurities from our minds. God is with us every step of the way and will guide us out to a place of freedom and abundance.

Prayer

It is comforting to know that as I go through these trying times in my first weeks, I know you are with me every step of the way, almighty God. I can move forward with absolute certainty that you are refining me, and this impurity in my mind will be released. I am confident I will feel the freedom and abundance you have planned for me, Father, during this refining process. Thank you, Jesus. Amen.

Daily Gratitude:

_____

_____

_____

_____

_____

_____

Reflections:

_____

_____

_____

_____

_____

_____

_____

_____

Day 6

Proverbs 4:14-15 (NASB)

Do not enter the path of the wicked
And do not proceed in the way of evil people.
Avoid it, do not pass by it;
Turn away from it and pass on.

Mindful Minute

We have reached this point because we realize our behavior has created a sinful habit in us.

We find ourselves in places and doing things we know are not in alignment with God's will for us. We say things we might not have otherwise said. We do things we may be ashamed of the next day. And we have the same conversations with ourselves daily while trying to navigate a new path, hoping we won't have to keep asking forgiveness for the same repeated behavior over and over again.

From this point forward, it's about being "all in" and not deviating from the path. We must succeed with determination and single-mindedness, putting one foot in front of the other during this time of exploring and committing to the path we believe we should follow moving forward. We must do what we need to do, removing the triggers long enough to find confidence in our ability to move forward with conviction about our choices.

We can, will, and should have faith in the promises of our Father so we can be set free from the spiritual battle that caused sin in us (turning away from God) and created the psychological slavery of what is now a life-interfering behavior/habit.

Prayer

Thank you for your wisdom, Father, in understanding where my weakness may lie. I look forward to the day when I will be able to confidently choose without a second thought because I have now found my strength in you. Please help me focus on removing as many distractions from my goal as possible and follow the path that leads to your will. With the power of your Spirit, I can avoid it, Father. I will be able to turn away from and pass on it. In Jesus' name I pray. Amen.

Daily Gratitude:

_____

_____

_____

_____

_____

_____

Reflections:

_____

_____

_____

_____

_____

_____

_____

_____

_____

Day 7

Matthew 5:13-16

You are the salt of the earth. But what good is salt if it has lost its flavor? Can you make it salty again? It will be thrown out and trampled underfoot as worthless. You are the light of the world—like a city on a hilltop that cannot be hidden. No one lights a lamp and then puts it under a basket. Instead, a lamp is placed on a stand, where it gives light to everyone in the house. In the same way, let your good deeds shine out for all to see, so that everyone will praise your heavenly Father.

Mindful Minute

Salt is a flavor enhancer that also delays decay. The natural progression in any system is toward decay or disorder unless acted on by an outside force.

Christians, being filled with a powerful divine force, can delay decay and shine light into this world. When we are consumed with behaviors or thoughts that interfere with our lives, our light can be dimmed, like it's hidden under a basket. Many times, our behaviors were done in the darkness and loneliness of our own homes. Other times, depending on the type of behavior, they were visible to all. Regardless of where we engaged, we must recognize how our behavior contributed to the decay of God's systems and dimmed our light because our minds were obsessed with thoughts not aligned with His Kingdom.

To love and follow Jesus is to desire to show His light. God created us as the salt of the earth, with value and purpose, meant to shine like a city on a hill. As we connect with others in daily life, they will see something different in us: peace and joy that defies human understanding, thereby provoking curiosity. We become a magnet for joy, gratefulness, and positivity.

Prayer

Father, thank you for this day and the opportunity to live a life where I can be free of the thoughts that have ensnared me. I recognize your Holy Spirit will allow me internal peace and, even more importantly, will allow your light to be seen by others. I can think of no greater gift of how to live my life. Thank you, Father, for offering your Son as the perfect sacrifice for wiping the slate clean on my past transgressions. I can now move forward with hope. In Jesus' name. Amen.

Daily Gratitude:

_____

_____

_____

_____

_____

_____

Reflections:

_____

_____

_____

_____

_____

_____

_____

_____

_____

Week 2: Days 8–14

Day 8

Isaiah 54:4

Fear not; you will no longer live in shame. Don't be afraid; there is no more disgrace for you. You will no longer remember the shame of your youth and the sorrows of widowhood.

Mindful Minute

The phrase "Fear not" is one of the most used expressions in the Bible, showing up hundreds of times, yet most of us allow fear to consume our thoughts. Shame produced by our toxic behaviors and sins of the past is real. Instead of understanding we may have done something wrong, we believe there is something wrong with us. As a result, we hide in the darkness fearing others might find out.

"Fear not" is a *command* and not a *request*. We can choose to ignore it and allow fear to grip our daily lives, or we can abide by it and trust in His promises. We have been forgiven, and we must obediently forgive ourselves. Let us take this thought of unforgiveness captive and simply agree with God. When we can do so, we become unencumbered by our past and are free to look at the world with wonderment and opportunity for the future.

Prayer

Thank you, Jesus, for suffering on the cross for me. I pray today to live in obedience to your Word and not allow the fear of the future or the shame of the past to dictate how I live my life. I trust you, Father. I agree with you. Despite feeling uncomfortable, I will stretch into this role and practice this new discipline. I know that living in the past prohibits me from seeing my potential in the future. In Jesus' mighty name. Amen.

Daily Gratitude:

_____

_____

_____

_____

_____

_____

Reflections:

_____

_____

_____

_____

_____

_____

_____

_____

Day 9

1 Corinthians 10:13

The temptations in your life are no different from what others experience. And God is faithful. He will not allow the temptation to be more than you can stand. When you are tempted, he will show you a way out so that you can endure.

Mindful Minute

It is easy to create a narrative for ourselves in terms of how difficult something can be, and "throw in the towel" because it is much easier than trying to "power through" this feeling of temptation.

The fact is that this life-interfering behavior and habit loop can cause temptation that might feel like more than we can bear for a moment. But by replacing the temptation with something positive, such as deep breathing, exercise, or any other redirection of activities, it *will* surely pass.

Consider going for a walk, calling a friend, reading a book, or cleaning the house to divert your attention. As this passage so clearly indicates, the temptations in your life are truly no different than what many others before you have tackled. When you are tempted, pause, breathe, redirect in some way, and trust God to show you a method in that moment.

Keep firmly in mind how He does have plans for you to prosper. Look beyond the *moment* to the life you so desire and a life in which He will say, "Well done, good and faithful servant."

Note: Download the free resource about the Lie Acronym at https://choosefreedom. today/free-resources

Prayer

Thank you, Father, for this day and reminder that the strength to make it through this and any moment of temptation is found through my choice to stop and recognize your presence, and truly know and understand that you are with me. This will surely pass, and you have a much better plan for me. In Jesus' name. Amen.

Daily Gratitude:

_____

_____

_____

_____

_____

_____

Reflections:

_____

_____

_____

_____

_____

_____

_____

_____

_____

Day 10

Proverbs 10:9

People with integrity walk safely, but those who follow crooked paths will
be exposed.

Mindful Minute

We are doing this challenge because somewhere along the way, we lost integrity with ourselves.

We told ourselves, and most likely God, how we wanted to stop something we knew was bad for us. We most likely knew there was a better life God saw for us without engaging in it. We promised ourselves over and over again, "This is the day I succeed." With each failed attempt came a loss of integrity in our word. Every time we promised ourselves something we could not deliver, there came an ever-so-small but noticeable impact on our self-esteem. It may not be so noticeable to the outside world, but it is something very evident to us and our loving Father.

The definition of the word "integrity," according to the Oxford dictionary, is "the state of being whole and undivided." Let us be whole and undivided as we fix our eyes on what lies ahead in place of the temptation we may feel today. The instruction in Proverbs 10:9 is so simple, yet many times it is admittedly much more difficult to accomplish. While there will be challenges, we are always capable of a mindset change when confronted with temptation. Each time distraction and temptation come knocking on our door, the opportunity for God's promise of something brighter in twelve weeks needs to enter our conscious thought.

Right now, the only goal is twelve weeks to give us the opportunity to see through a new set of eyes the promises God has made to us when released from this psychological slavery.

Prayer

Thank you, Father, for this simple instruction today. I want to have integrity with myself and with you over these twelve weeks because I trust in your promises to see the person I am fully capable of being without the psychological slavery of this habit. In Jesus' name. Amen.

Daily Gratitude:

_____

_____

_____

_____

_____

_____

Reflections:

_____

_____

_____

_____

_____

_____

_____

_____

_____

Day 11

Ephesians 6:10-11

A final word: Be strong in the Lord and in his mighty power. Put on all of God's armor so that you will be able to stand firm against all strategies of the devil.

Mindful Minute

If you've been a Christian for some time, chances are good you're familiar with this verse. God's Word has much wisdom and instruction for how to live our lives.

When it comes to life-interfering behaviors that are not in line with God's will, the devil has many strategies to derail our efforts. When we look at the reasons we re-engaged in the past, we become aware of just how cunning he has been in tripping us up. During these twelve weeks, we will be able to put ourselves in many situations where we can stand firm against the strategies of the devil. We do not always have the luxury of knowing when temptation will come, but we can have a good idea of the times and places they may occur.

When we can anticipate our triggers, we can develop a plan. The plan starts with this verse and prayer. God's armor elicits a picture of great strength, and we wear it with faith that we will see this through to victory. Run the film to the end of the temptation, and envision how you will come out of the situation on the other side of your choice.

Be honest with yourself about the most likely course of events following a choice to entertain this behavior. Conversely, picture how great you will feel about having integrity with yourself and God when you choose to persevere. When we envision the result, we have a direction to go.

Prayer

I am ready, Father, with a plan to thwart the cunning strategies of the enemy. Readily aware of the consequences, I will develop a strategy to get to the other side. I know my confidence will increase each time I practice, and I will build integrity with myself. In Jesus' name. Amen.

Daily Gratitude:

_____

_____

_____

_____

_____

_____

Reflections:

_____

_____

_____

_____

_____

_____

_____

_____

_____

Day 12

1 Corinthians 9:24

Don't you realize that in a race everyone runs, but only one person gets the prize? So run to win!

Mindful Minute

We are taking this challenge because there is a behavioral habit that has taken control of our lives in a significant and sometimes debilitating way.

Changing behavior takes preparation and training, just as any runner knows preparation and training are required to successfully complete a race. Oxford's definition of the verb race is, "Compete with another or others to see who is fastest at covering a set course or achieving an objective." Our focus in this verse relates to *how* we will run the race we choose to enter.

We have committed to this race called twelve weeks of freedom from a life-interfering behavior. The purpose is to remove the habit that has created havoc in our lives so we may experience a new and better way of living. The behavior has become an idol in our life, holding a place more important to us than our relationship with God.

Our godly instruction for the race we choose to enter is that we must "run to win." We are in this for the prize of seeing who we get to become and who we were intended to be from our Creator's perspective after removing this harmful behavior.

Prayer

Father, in this race for twelve weeks of freedom from this behavior that has caused me to lose integrity with myself, I am committed to running this race for the *win*. I will keep my eyes focused straight ahead as I know you have better plans for me. In Jesus' mighty name. Amen.

Daily Gratitude:

_____

_____

_____

_____

_____

_____

Reflections:

_____

_____

_____

_____

_____

_____

_____

_____

_____

Day 13

Isaiah 43:19

For I am about to do something new. See, I have already begun! Do you not see it? I will make a pathway through the wilderness. I will create rivers in the dry wasteland.

Mindful Minute

In Isaiah 43, God talked to his people who had just been released from exile. Isaiah explained that to experience a renewal, Judah needed to turn away from its sinful ways.

God creates the pathway from wasteland to rivers! God loves us and sees each one of us not for how we fall short but for all the potential we have to provide light to others. Each of us is uniquely gifted with something extraordinary that has been hidden and locked up, exiled, by our habit.

As we walk this path of changing our sinful and life-interfering behavior, we can rest assured that God is creating something new in us. Hope that God is finding the person he created us to be provides powerful motivation for us to persevere.

Prayer

Thank you, Father. I was created for something more, yet I am discouraged when this sinful behavior gets in the way of realizing my full potential. Today, I trust in you to provide the path for me to walk and find the "me" you created me to be. I will walk in faith. Thank you, Jesus, for paying the price for my prior sin. Amen.

Daily Gratitude:

_____

_____

_____

_____

_____

_____

Reflections:

_____

_____

_____

_____

_____

_____

_____

_____

Day 14

Proverbs 4:25-27

Look straight ahead and fix your eyes on what lies before you. Mark out a straight path for your feet; stay on the safe path. Don't get sidetracked; keep your feet from following evil.

Mindful Minute

God makes a path for us out of the wilderness. He will help when we are tempted.

We stand today in faith and with certainty that God knows the ending to this story should we choose to not get distracted. He knows the end even when we do get distracted. The timing of when things are revealed to us is in His hands. It will not always coincide with the timing we have in mind for ourselves, and there will certainly be frustration, anxiety, and temptations along the way.

The enemy will have a story that is meant to sidetrack us. Let us keep our eyes on the prize and remember we are training and running the race to win. The instructions for today are clear. "Look straight ahead and fix your eyes on what lies before you. Don't get sidetracked."

The only one way to see something different, is to follow Him. Rely on the Holy Spirit's strength and His plan when we feel tempted.

Prayer

Thank you, Father, for I am restored in your Word as I commit to stay on the path you provided to ensure I get out of the wilderness where I have been lost. I desire the freedom to see the possibilities and plans. Thank you, Jesus. Amen.

Daily Gratitude:

_____

_____

_____

_____

_____

_____

Reflections:

_____

_____

_____

_____

_____

_____

_____

_____

_____

Week 3: Days 15–21

Day 15

James 1:2-4

Dear brothers and sisters, when troubles of any kind come your way, consider it an opportunity for great joy. For you know that when your faith is tested, your endurance has a chance to grow. So let it grow, for when your endurance is fully developed, you will be perfect and complete, needing nothing.

Mindful Minute

Though written almost 2,000 years ago, this verse perfectly describes the current science of the brain for building new habits in our unconscious mind when we battle anything as a result of habitual sin or something that has become a life-interfering behavior.

The interesting part of this instruction in today's verse is to "consider it an opportunity for great joy" whenever trouble comes along. The reason we can be joyful about processing difficult or painful temptations is that once we endure, we have a chance to form a new neurological habit and grow from it.

Each time we succeed in diverting the temptation into something different, we form a new neural pathway that gets us out of the psychological slavery we have been accustomed to. That is surely a reason to be joyful!

Prayer

Thank you, Father, for this instruction. As I encounter difficult moments or temptation, I will remember to look at this as an opportunity to be joyful about the future once I rid myself of this habit and behavior that created havoc in my life. I will look for alternative ways to deal with the stress of the moment. Thank you, Jesus. Amen.

Daily Gratitude:

_____

_____

_____

_____

_____

_____

Reflections:

_____

_____

_____

_____

_____

_____

_____

_____

Day 16

James 1:12

God blesses those who patiently endure testing and temptation. Afterward they will receive the crown of life that God has promised to those who love him.

Mindful Minute

In the first Chapter of James, he is talking to a group of Jewish believers, telling them that when their faith is tested, to consider it great joy. Verse 3 states, "For you know when your faith is tested, your endurance has a chance to grow."

According to verse 12, we understand that patience is needed when we are faced with temptation. We can patiently wait as the temptation processes through our thoughts and the stress of the temptation exits our bodies. In this case, make sure to practice and use the LIE Acronym (Download the free resource about the LIE acronym at https://choosefreedom.today/free-resources).

We need to be patient as we walk through 84 consecutive days of capturing our thoughts and making them obedient to God and His plan for us.

Life is not easy. It's not easy for believers and it's not easy for unbelievers. The difference for us, as believers, is that we are running this race called life and persevering through temptations. We do this because we know what awaits us is the promise of freedom in Christ (Galatians 5:1) while we are here on earth, and the promise of an eternal life with our Lord and Savior.

Practicing gratitude, prayer, and meditation on His Word each day helps us create new neurological pathways that make it easier to resist temptation as we go through life. We will be rewarded with freedom from the psychological slavery we have been enduring. We will be rewarded with the confidence of our eternal destiny.

Prayer

Thank you, Lord, for your continued instruction to persevere to experience your blessings. I want to live a life of gratitude, always remembering what you suffered for me to have hope in the future. In Jesus' name. Amen.

Daily Gratitude:

_____

_____

_____

_____

_____

_____

_____

Reflections:

_____

_____

_____

_____

_____

_____

_____

_____

_____

_____

Day 17

Ephesians 4:22-24

Throw off your old sinful nature and your former way of life, which is corrupted by lust and deception. Instead, let the Spirit renew your thoughts and attitudes. Put on your new nature, created to be like God—truly righteous and holy.

Mindful Minute

There is a consequence we are suffering as a result of *lust and deception* in something dealing with worldly desires.

We were deceived into believing relaxation, comfort, and peace came from the pleasures of this world. We now have a rearview mirror to reflect on the deception that those pleasures represented because of the psychological slavery they created within us. The good news is that our thoughts and attitudes can and will be shifted by focusing our attention on God and allowing the Spirit to renew them.

We do this by being in His Word daily, meditating on Scripture, and reflecting on the wisdom embedded there. Being led by the Holy Spirit is freeing and allows us to experience the new nature He offered to us by trusting in Him. Our faith in the work that Jesus did on the cross creates righteousness and holiness in us.

Holiness simply means that we have been set apart for a higher moral purpose, and righteousness means that we have been morally set apart because of the work Jesus did on the cross. Praise God for these gifts given to us by grace.

Prayer

Father, I do want to throw off my old sinful nature regarding this behavior that has created sin in me. I acknowledge that a very deceptive way of thinking was involved in my reasons for engaging. I understand how this habit created sin in my life. I want a renewed mind and way of thinking. I look forward to the future and my new nature as I walk this path with you. Thank you, Jesus, for paying the price for my past sins and creating holiness and righteousness within me. I want to honor you in my walk today. Amen.

Daily Gratitude:

_____

_____

_____

_____

_____

_____

Reflections:

_____

_____

_____

_____

_____

_____

_____

_____

_____

Day 18

Psalm 86:11

Teach me your ways, O Lord, that I may live according to your truth! Grant me purity of heart, so that I honor you.

Mindful Minute

As we pause our participation in a life-interfering behavior during these twelve weeks, we have an opportunity to divert our attention to something good and positive.

We can take the time to get to know God better and understand that in His creation, He made everything good. Using our daily journal to list out what we are grateful for and meditating on His Word creates closeness, understanding of His loving nature, and His wonderful plan for us. This ultimately makes it easier to abide in His ways and His love. The more we understand the depth of His love, the more we want to abide in His ways.

As we grow closer to Him and understand His incredible love for us, we develop a healthy fear of being disconnected from Him. This is how we start to understand just how much He desires us to avoid situations that steal our relationships, productivity, and identity.

The natural product of healthy fear is experiencing the beauty, awe, and love of our Heavenly Father.

Prayer

Father, thank you for your Word today. I thank you for everything in my life that is good and give all the glory to you. Continue to teach me your ways through Scripture so I can draw closer to you. Thank you, Jesus. Amen.

Daily Gratitude:

_____

_____

_____

_____

_____

_____

Reflections:

_____

_____

_____

_____

_____

_____

_____

_____

_____

Day 19

Proverbs 2:2-4

Tune your ears to wisdom and concentrate on understanding. Cry out for insight and ask for understanding. Search for them as you would for silver; seek them like hidden treasures.

Mindful Minute

People talk about the wisdom embedded in the Bible. They trust biblical wisdom yet have no faith in God. Why wouldn't we want to follow the One who provides wisdom?

As humans, we have certainly become adept at following people without it. Why haven't we focused on the Bible more since it gives us such great wisdom and insight? During these twelve weeks, we are training ourselves to spend more time in God's Word, reflecting on the wisdom of our Heavenly Father. We begin to understand, see, and document how we ignored His loving instruction and took matters into our own hands. We will realize the consequences of discounting the most powerful wisdom we could have ever comprehended.

These verses urge us to seek wisdom as earnestly as we would search for silver or hidden treasures. Can you imagine if we seek wisdom the same way we would seek financial success? Can you imagine seeking wisdom as if you were on a real-life treasure hunt?

Let us cling to God's Word on a daily basis to know and experience the wisdom our Heavenly Father gives, to live our best lives and to be free of the psychological slavery that has been created by stepping outside of biblical wisdom.

Prayer

Heavenly Father, I seek your wisdom. I want to walk with you daily, and even hourly, because I know I will experience temptation to walk away from you. I desire wisdom to make choices to live my most authentic life. I know your wisdom provides the best path for my life. I desire people to see your Spirit inside me as I begin to choose wisely and experience the results of that wisdom. Thank you, Jesus, for your sacrifice on the cross so that I might live in freedom. In Jesus' name. Amen.

Daily Gratitude:

_____

_____

_____

_____

_____

_____

Reflections:

_____

_____

_____

_____

_____

_____

_____

_____

Day 20

Galatians 6:9

So let's not get tired of doing what is good. At just the right time we will reap a harvest of blessing if we don't give up.

Mindful Minute

We have been doing this journey long enough to see the benefits of putting our life-interfering behavior to the side.

We find more time in the day to accomplish our goals. We might use that time to attend to some self-care or something that was on our list of things to do that never got done. We develop confidence in our ability to let our *no* be no. We are developing integrity with our word! The Holy Spirit may be more present in our conversations.

It is important to document our progress as we go through this process. As today's Scripture guides us, we must not get tired of doing what is good for ourselves and our bodies. We don't give up. Our hope in Christ and His promises of reaping a harvest is key to staying on this path.

Prayer

Heavenly Father, thank you for this beautiful day. I recognize all that has transpired in this short time by putting my sinful habit to the side and allowing my body and mind to heal. I look forward to the harvests I shall reap during this journey of freeing myself from psychological slavery. Thank you, Jesus. Amen.

Daily Gratitude:

_____

_____

_____

_____

_____

Reflections:

_____

_____

_____

_____

_____

_____

_____

_____

Day 21

John 16:33

I have told you all this so that you may have peace in me. Here on earth, you will have many trials and sorrows. But take heart because I have overcome the world.

Mindful Minute

For many, this life-interfering behavior formed over a long period of time.

It may have started out innocently enough as we told ourselves it was okay to engage because it created an escape from the stressors of everyday life. We were looking for peace in something that was of this world and turned our attention away from God.

God has a plan, and we trust He is in control. We can gain the peace that surpasses human understanding. We find different mechanisms to cope with the trials and sorrows of this world and consider alternative strategies in place of our old habits.

Make sure you are diligent to replace the old habit/behavior with a new one. Breathe, meditate on God's Word, pray, or engage with someone you want to connect with. Divert your attention to something productive. Over time, with the help of the Holy Spirit, these things will become a new habit to deal with the stresses and anxieties of life.

Prayer

Father, grant peace as I walk through trying times. You have already written the ending, and I know you use all things for good for those who love you. I love you, Father. I will trust in you as I walk this path and meditate on your Word each day. Thank you, Jesus. Amen.

Daily Gratitude:

_____

_____

_____

_____

_____

_____

Reflections:

_____

_____

_____

_____

_____

_____

_____

_____

_____

Week 4: Days 22–28

Day 22

2 Corinthians 10:5 (NIV)

We demolish arguments and every pretension that sets itself up against the knowledge of God, and we take captive every thought to make it obedient to Christ.

Mindful Minute

As far as spiritual battles go, there may not be a more appropriate verse to help us be aware of the enemy's strategy to get us off course.

It most likely took years to get to this point where we said, "Enough is enough." We felt ready to see how we could change things. We committed to walking with God through a journey for twelve weeks, and, for some, beyond. We see change. Excited to see something different, we believe God has a better plan.

But just when we feel better, a thought comes into play. "Just this once," or "No one will know." Beware, because *there it is*! It is a thought that leads us away from our commitment and away from God's plan. That thought allows us to lose integrity with ourselves, and maybe with others as well. It is certainly a thought that will allow us to lose our obedience to following Jesus.

This version of the verse is my favorite because it speaks to "demolishing" the thought. The visualization is like taking a wrecking ball to it! Scripture gives the perfect example of what happens when we engage with something that is in conflict with God's will. Once Eve entertained having a conversation with the enemy, she engaged with a dangerous adversary who told her choosing to disobey would make things better.

Don't believe the lie. Demolish and redirect the thought towards Christ. For more information about using the LIE Acronym when tempted, see the free resources at https://choosefreedom.today/free-resources.

Prayer

Father, thank you for this reminder. It can be easy to give up and be led astray when things get easier. I don't want to believe the lies of the enemy. I want to focus on what your plans are for me when I get to the other side of this and can freely choose with confidence the path you've prepared for me. I want to capture the thoughts that are not in alignment with you and redirect them toward you. Thank you, Jesus. Amen.

Daily Gratitude:

_____

_____

_____

_____

_____

_____

Reflections:

_____

_____

_____

_____

_____

_____

_____

_____

_____

Day 23

Romans 12:12

Rejoice in our confident hope. Be patient in trouble, and keep on praying.

Mindful Minute

As Christians, we can put our faith in Jesus and have a never-ending source of hope. Setting aside time each day for prayer and gratitude allows us to always be in His presence and know He has a better plan for us.

Science has repeatedly confirmed God's Word in the area of gratitude. People who practice seeing the good in things with an attitude of solving problems with a positive rather than negative mindset have hope for something better. They access a part of the brain that processes empathy, compassion, and creativity. These are the powerful qualities that exist in the life of someone who trusts God and rejoices in a confident hope.

Whether we are a spectator or participant, life will always include a series of troubles and unsettling experiences alongside contentment and joy. When we have hope, we can be patient and endure.

When we have gratitude for all that is good and comes from God in this world, we can see opportunity in every situation. When we pray, we feel His presence and have confidence in His love. Let us have confident hope as we navigate this twelve-week path and beyond.

Prayer

Father, I pray today for unwavering hope. I will walk this path knowing there is something better. I will believe this despite all the challenges and difficulties that may come my way. I will breathe and meditate on your Word and pray to develop the patience needed to see the gift of living life full of hope despite my circumstances. Thank you, Jesus. Amen.

Daily Gratitude:

_____

_____

_____

_____

_____

_____

_____

Reflections:

_____

_____

_____

_____

_____

_____

_____

_____

_____

Day 24

Romans 15:4

Such things were written in the Scriptures long ago to teach us. And the Scriptures give us hope and encouragement as we wait patiently for God's promises to be fulfilled.

Mindful Minute

We have used quotes from the book of Romans several times so far during our first four weeks. This is for good reason when you understand the purpose of Romans against the backdrop of the entirety of the Bible.

The book of Romans was written by the Apostle Paul to summarize the Good News about Jesus Christ. The New Testament book explains the human condition and the meaning of life while we are on this earth. It gives guidance to followers of Christ on how to deal with the problems, failures, and disputes characterized by life in this world.

We can easily confirm why so many verses are directly applicable to our journey in this twelve-week process. All of Scripture is the basis for building a story to teach us. God has had a plan since the beginning of time. He left us with the Helper, the Holy Spirit, so we will never feel alone in our walk.

While we may be surrounded by sin and temptation, we can remain hopeful in His loving instruction that God has a different and better plan for us. With this hope and encouragement, we can stay strong in our walk with Him.

Prayer

Father, I am grateful today for your unconditional love and instruction. Thank you for reminding me of your faithfulness to all of humanity. You have a purpose and a plan, have provided Jesus as the ultimate sacrifice, and left us with our Helper, the Holy Spirit, as a mechanism for all to wait patiently as we witness your plan unfold. I remain steadfast and patient with joyful anticipation. Thank you, Jesus. Amen.

Daily Gratitude:

_____

_____

_____

_____

_____

_____

Reflections:

_____

_____

_____

_____

_____

_____

_____

_____

Day 25

Romans 13:12

The night is almost gone; the day of salvation will soon be here. So remove your dark deeds like dirty clothes and put on the shining armor of right living.

Mindful Minute

If we desire something new, we are reminded how important it is to start living right and remove those things done in the darkness.

The metaphor is perfect as we consider how it feels to remove dirty clothes from our bodies. Removing bad habits makes us feel *clean* and *new*. This is where transformation begins!

When we can reflect upon our life-interfering behavior with a clear mind, we start to understand the deception behind our relationship with it. Compare it to the deception that took place in the Garden of Eden with Adam and Eve. Do we ultimately find the relaxation or connection that we truly desire when we engage, or does engaging give us regret the next day? Does engaging decrease our anxiety as we had anticipated, or did it increase because of the guilt and shame it created?

If we are honest with ourselves, this behavior is stealing precious time to truly connect with others, to address life's problems in a healthy manner, and to live the life God intended for us.

Prayer

Father, I am keenly aware of your ultimate plan to defeat the evil one. I desire to be in your love with the light of the Holy Spirit so others may see and follow suit. I want to rid my body of these dirty clothes. I want to be unencumbered by the psychological slavery of this habit. I so very much desire the shining armor of right living for all to see. Thank you, Jesus. Amen.

Daily Gratitude:

_____

_____

_____

_____

_____

_____

Reflections:

_____

_____

_____

_____

_____

_____

_____

_____

_____

Day 26

Galatians 5:13

For you have been called to live in freedom, my brothers and sisters. But don't use your freedom to satisfy your sinful nature. Instead, use your freedom to serve one another in love. For the whole law can be summed up in this one command: "Love your neighbor as yourself."

Mindful Minute

God has always given us the ability and freedom to choose our own path.

He left us with the Holy Spirit to discern good from evil. The habit cycle that led to our need to be here today created psychological slavery, the opposite of freedom. Freeing the time we spent in the past on this habit gives us the opportunity to create new ones.

Time spent engaging in this life-interfering behavior took us away from being present with ourselves and others. It did not give us the promised relaxation, enjoyment, or a solution to a problem we faced. What self-care habits could you consider incorporating into your life that remind you that *you matter*? It should be something that provides authentic peace, relaxation, and joy. When we practice love and care for ourselves, it is easier to love and care for others.

Prayer

Father, thank you for the freedom to choose. Today, I choose you and want to spend more time on self-care and self-love for the purpose of loving those around me more passionately. I want the Holy Spirit to be experienced through me. Thank you, Jesus. In your name I pray. Amen.

Daily Gratitude:

_____

_____

_____

_____

_____

_____

Reflections:

_____

_____

_____

_____

_____

_____

_____

_____

_____

Day 27

Ezekiel 2:2

The Spirit came into me as he spoke, and he set me on my feet. I listened carefully to his words.

Mindful Minute

When we are believers, we have access to the Holy Spirit who speaks directly to us.

Believers can know His voice intimately, but we might not have acknowledged it as much as we'd like to admit. Most likely, we've been hearing His voice for years regarding our habit. Perhaps you've heard Him say, "I promise your life will be so much more fulfilled without continued engagement in this repeated behavior."

We can misinterpret Scripture as a bunch of rules to follow, restricting us from living a full life. Yet, by our choices, and in hindsight, we can see how His loving voice and instruction were and are meant for good. It is meant to protect us from poor decision-making.

As we walk through this journey of twelve weeks or beyond, remember His wisdom when things get tough. Let us carefully hear His words when tempted. Let us remember His love for us. Let us remember He has a better plan for us.

Prayer

Father, I want to listen *carefully* to your words, this day and every other. I want to focus on your loving instruction and abide in the joy of your love. I want to develop a desire to be in your presence continually, such that I am a slave to your ways, not the ways of this world. In Jesus' mighty name. Amen.

Daily Gratitude:

_____

_____

_____

_____

_____

_____

Reflections:

_____

_____

_____

_____

_____

_____

_____

_____

_____

Day 28

James 1:5-6

If you need wisdom, ask our generous God, and he will give it to you. He will not rebuke you for asking. But when you ask him, be sure that your faith is in God alone. Do not waver, for a person with divided loyalty is as unsettled as a wave of the sea that is blown and tossed by the wind.

Mindful Minute

A lot of wisdom is required to understand the consequences of our choices regarding our bad habit. We certainly possess enough personal wisdom to understand the consequences of engaging in it.

Godly wisdom is something different. It involves going outside of ourselves to understand and feel the depth of His love and trust that there is a better plan for us.

As far as our habit and life-interfering behavior is concerned, we can commit to undivided loyalty moving forward. Unhindered faith is trust that produces action. Once we allow a divided loyalty to this or any other life-interfering behavior or habit, we feel unsettled, and *struggle* sets in.

The picture of being tossed at sea is a powerful analogy. Instead, we ask God for His wisdom as we navigate this path called life.

Prayer

Heavenly Father, I thank you for allowing me to access your godly wisdom. I do not wish to feel like I am tossed at sea. If tempted, I will look up with great faith and not waver. I know there is a better plan, and I cannot wait to experience it. Thank you, Jesus, for your great sacrifice so I can move forward and not be encumbered by what is behind me. Amen.

Daily Gratitude:

_____

_____

_____

_____

_____

_____

_____

Reflections:

_____

_____

_____

_____

_____

_____

_____

_____

_____

Week 5: Days 29-35

Day 29

1 Corinthians 15:58

So, my dear brothers and sisters, be strong and immovable. Always work enthusiastically for the Lord, for you know that nothing you do for the Lord is ever useless.

Mindful Minute

This part of Paul's letter to the Corinthians is his proclamation that Christ rose from the dead. He mentions the many who witnessed the event. Paul notes his own amazement that he saw Christ and is now called an apostle.

Paul explains how if we do not believe, we cannot hope for a future resurrection ourselves. Paul describes his personal unworthiness because, prior to meeting the resurrected Jesus in person, Paul persecuted many who believed in Jesus.

Paul understood the depth of love and forgiveness embodied in this act of sacrifice, and spent his life proclaiming this truth. He went on to write more than half the books of the New Testament. If Paul, a murderer of those who loved Jesus, can be forgiven and have this much impact on the world, surely God can use us to influence others in our lifetime through our own light.

Our self-sabotaging thoughts reduce our ability to influence others for Christ. The instruction to "work enthusiastically for the Lord" is applicable in our journey, as well as remembering "nothing you do for the Lord is ever useless."

Forgive yourself, be strong, and believe all of your gifts, hurts, and experiences will ultimately be used for His Glory.

Prayer

Father, I want to be steadfast, immovable, and see the picture of myself that you see. I want to know that my walk is not in vain. I want to be freed from the chains of this slavery and be your witness to true internal and external joy. Thank you, Jesus, for your sacrifice so I can look forward to a life you can use for your glory. Amen.

Daily Gratitude:

_____

_____

_____

_____

_____

_____

Reflections:

_____

_____

_____

_____

_____

_____

_____

_____

_____

Day 30

Psalm 23:3

He renews my strength. He guides me along right paths, bringing honor
to his name.

Mindful Minute

Day 30 is a celebration of a meaningful milestone. Congratulations! We have walked
daily in the path of His Word, focusing on His loving instruction as we met the challenges and temptations laid before us.

The enemy is cunning, and will not cease trying to divert our attention to a destructive path that looks more romantic than it is. Think about the deception in the
Garden. Adam and Eve could have all the fruit freely in the Garden *except* from one
tree. They had everything they needed and only had to resist one. God was guiding
them along the right path, yet the serpent was cunning enough to convince them
that He was holding something back from them.

Through this twelve-week walk, we are building a new neural pathway and habit so
we continue to lessen the voice and impact of the enemy. The enemy does not go
away, but through practice and with the help of the Holy Spirit, his voice has less
and less power over us. The more we practice putting on the armor of God over the
darkness, the more the light of the Holy Spirit is evident within us.

It is a felt experience that grows stronger as we continue to look forward to what
future is possible without the psychological slavery associated with this repeated
life-interfering behavior.

Prayer

Thank you, Father. I rejoice in this victory that has been provided by virtue of your
loving instruction and the sacrifice of your Son. I desire to continue this journey to
renew my strength and bring honor to you through the shining light of the Holy
Spirit. In Jesus' name. Amen.

Daily Gratitude:

_____

_____

_____

_____

_____

_____

Reflections:

_____

_____

_____

_____

_____

_____

_____

_____

_____

Day 31

Matthew 11:28-30

Then Jesus said, "Come to me, all of you who are weary and carry heavy burdens, and I will give you rest. Take my yoke upon you. Let me teach you, because I am humble and gentle at heart, and you will find rest for your souls. For my yoke is easy to bear, and the burden I give you is light."

Mindful Minute

If we have been in the devotional daily, we have practiced meditation on Scripture, prayer, and gratitude each day. As we transition into the next part of our journey, we are reminded through this verse of where we can find true peace and *rest* for our souls.

The world is a fast-paced place filled with ways that make it easy to distract ourselves from the truly important things in life. As we continue to make time for Him, we find more peace throughout our day. Time with God is a self-care practice. The Lord's prayer reminds us to depend on God for our needs for the day. This thought alone should provide some mechanism of peace if we trust Him for what we need.

Consider other ways the Holy Spirit may reflect something greater within us through self-care practices. While this may seem selfish, exhibiting a restful spirit with Him inspires and helps others to be restful.

What practices of self-care could you start during this next stage in your journey to help you with the concept of *rest* and peace for yourself? Consider a new habit of self-care today that is realistic, measurable, and achievable.

Prayer

I desire a restful spirit, Father, and I thank you for your Word each day that inspires and encourages me. I will meditate here with you to allow the Holy Spirit to speak within me so I know where to focus and make my burden lighter. Thank you, Jesus. Amen.

Daily Gratitude:

_____

_____

_____

_____

_____

_____

Reflections:

_____

_____

_____

_____

_____

_____

_____

_____

_____

Day 32

1 Peter 4:12-13

Dear friends, don't be surprised at the fiery trials you are going through, as if something strange were happening to you. Instead, be very glad—for these trials make you partners with Christ in his suffering, so that you will have the wonderful joy of seeing his glory when it is revealed to all the world.

Mindful Minute

There are so many verses worthy of inscribing into our hearts, and this one is no exception, not only for this twelve-week period but for a lifetime. In this passage, Peter is warning those who follow Christ to expect fiery trials. In Peter's time, intense political and social persecution would come to those who proclaimed Christ's name. In most countries today, it's not so dangerous to be a Christian. Fiery trials, however, are indeed a normal part of life on this earth, especially when one proclaims Jesus as their Lord and Savior.

According to Ephesians 2:2 (NIV), Satan is described as "…the ruler of the kingdom of the air, the spirit who is now at work in those who are disobedient." Because of sin in this world, we must not get too comfortable with our daily walk. We must also be prepared for things that try us both emotionally and physically. When we can accept the fact that life will throw many heartbreaking surprises at us, we can mentally prepare for them. Develop a plan to defeat the enemy, expecting the unexpected at any time so we can identify it and be ready to respond.

Prayer

Father, I will not be surprised when things become more difficult than I want. I want to remember that in all trials, I can find my strength in you. I know I will not have to endure more than I can handle, and I will be the victor to reveal my true strength in you. Thank you, Jesus. Amen.

Daily Gratitude:

_____

_____

_____

_____

_____

_____

Reflections:

_____

_____

_____

_____

_____

_____

_____

_____

Day 33

Ephesians 6:13-17

Therefore, put on every piece of God's armor so you will be able to resist the enemy in the time of evil. Then after the battle you will still be standing firm. Stand your ground, putting on the belt of truth and the body armor of God's righteousness. For shoes, put on the peace that comes from the Good News so that you will be fully prepared. In addition to all of these, hold up the shield of faith to stop the fiery arrows of the devil. Put on salvation as your helmet, and take the sword of the Spirit, which is the word of God.

Mindful Minute

Yesterday we reflected on being prepared for fiery trials. Knowing they will come is of primary importance. Having adequate protections in place is critical through such trials. Putting on the "whole armor" of God means not allowing any part of ourselves to be exposed to Satan (eyes, ears, tongue, feet, etc.) The belt of truth is the first place we should go as we "armor up" against the enemy's schemes. While there are several truths we could list, the first one that should come to mind is the truth about the effects that our life-interfering behavior has had on us.

We committed to this twelve-week program because we have been doing something repeatedly that has not been serving us. It was getting in the way of us living and experiencing the life God intended. Will engaging in it provide us with the solace we truly desire, or is this a scheme of deception like the one in the Garden of Eden? This verse also discusses the "peace" that comes from the Good News.

Jesus is the Good News for Christians because He died on the cross for our sins. Peace is the goal, and peace is what we have when we rely on His promises. Faith in Him gives us hope for a better future and *peace* despite circumstances. Keep His Word in your heart and use it as your sword.

Prayer

I want to be ready for any trial, Father. Thank you, Jesus, for dying on the cross and giving me hope in your ultimate plan. Thank you for the tools of truth in your Word. I will place them in my heart so the enemy's deception will not prevail. I will practice wearing the full armor of God by standing firm. Thank you, Jesus. Amen.

Daily Gratitude:

_____

_____

_____

_____

_____

_____

_____

Reflections:

_____

_____

_____

_____

_____

_____

_____

_____

_____

Day 34

Psalm 1:1-3

Oh, the joys of those who do not follow the advice of the wicked, or stand around with sinners, or join in with mockers. But they delight in the law of the Lord, meditating on it day and night. They are like trees planted along the riverbank, bearing fruit each season. Their leaves never wither, and they prosper in all they do.

Mindful Minute

When we are trying to redirect a habit that has overtaken us, it is important to consider who we spend our time with. There is a saying: "Show me your friends, and I will show you your future." There is biblical wisdom behind that. In psychology, it is known as the chameleon effect, which refers to our tendency to unconsciously mirror the behaviors of others. This happens because we are wired for connection, and we often adapt our behavior to strengthen those social bonds.

If we want to change something that we know is not serving us, we must intentionally surround ourselves with people whose lives reflect the direction we want to go. That does not mean leaving others behind. Jesus lived among sinners, and we all fall short. But it does mean seeking out relationships that lift us up and draw us closer to the person God created us to be. Volunteering at your church or getting involved in a cause you care about can help you meet people who inspire growth.

This transformation is not instant, but it is essential. Psalm 1 reminds us of the joy and stability that come from delighting in God's Word and aligning ourselves with His truth. As we make wiser choices about the people we surround ourselves with, we begin to see the fruit of that decision in every area of our lives.

Prayer

Father, I live to prosper in the joy of knowing you and choosing not to get in the way of myself. I meditate this morning on your Word so my life will not wither but instead reflect a light that shines so brightly, it leads others to you. Thank you, Jesus. Amen.

Daily Gratitude:

_____

_____

_____

_____

_____

_____

Reflections:

_____

_____

_____

_____

_____

_____

_____

_____

_____

Day 35

1 Corinthians 6:19

Don't you realize that your body is the temple of the Holy Spirit, who lives in you and was given to you by God? You do not belong to yourself.

Mindful Minute

The history of God's presence (and temple) starts in the Garden of Eden with Adam and Eve. God has always intended to be in a close and personal relationship with us as was shown in the Garden. After the fall of Adam and Eve, God still desired a close and personal relationship with His people and used the portable tabernacle (as described in the book of Exodus) to be in the presence of His people. After reaching the promised land in Jerusalem, God assigned the task of building the temple to Solomon, David's son. Once again, God was in relationship with His people through this temple. The temple built by Solomon was completed and then later destroyed by the Babylonians, though years later, another temple would be built by His people.

Upon Jesus's death, the curtains of the temple in Jerusalem were ripped in two as a sign that this form of worship had ended. After His resurrection and ascension to Heaven, we are told in John 14 that Jesus sent a Helper in His place, which is the Spirit of Truth. This Spirit lives within us and therefore makes our very bodies God's Temple, used as a means to be in close relationship with Him. Everything you do as a believer is done in the presence of God. How does it change your perception of yourself to know that you are a Holy dwelling place for God's presence?

Prayer

Father, thank you for sending the Holy Spirit to dwell within me so I will never be alone. Help me remain mindful of His voice and presence, making choices that protect your temple and keep my heart open to your guidance. I want to live in joy and light. In Jesus' name. Amen.

Daily Gratitude:

_____

_____

_____

_____

_____

_____

Reflections:

_____

_____

_____

_____

_____

_____

_____

_____

Week 6: Days 36-42

Day 36

1 Chronicles 28:20

Then David continued, "Be strong and courageous, and do the work. Don't be afraid or discouraged, for the Lord God, my God, is with you. He will not fail you or forsake you. He will see to it that all the work related to the Temple of the Lord is finished correctly."

Mindful Minute

This verse is so powerful in its simplicity. A godly man (David) telling his godly son (Solomon) to "do the work." There was a monumental task ahead in building a temple for God, and Solomon was told to "do the work."

So many times, we default to asking God to just make something better without our own involvement. We want a miracle without any work on our part. God is certainly capable of miracles, but as we have seen through the Scripture we have been reviewing in this devotional thus far, He also often asks us to "do the work" and "stay the course." Accountability on our part is required when we follow Him, and in return, we are promised something better. We are reminded here, though, that we are never alone in our journey. He is with us, and He will not fail us or forsake us.

Let us remember that in creating a new neural pathway for better habits, we must be highly engaged in *doing the work* with the Holy Spirit as our guide and our strength.

Prayer

Thank you for this reminder, Lord, that I find my strength in you and that I absolutely can have confidence that you are with me and will see me through to the end. I will do the work so I may experience the full power of your beautiful temple within me through the Holy Spirit. Thank you. In Jesus mighty name. Amen.

Daily Gratitude:

_____

_____

_____

_____

_____

_____

Reflections:

_____

_____

_____

_____

_____

_____

_____

_____

_____

Day 37

Colossians 4:2

Devote yourselves to prayer with an alert mind and a thankful heart.

Mindful Minute

Today's verse is simple yet packed with powerful wisdom. Continue to look up and thank God for all that is good in the world. Pray in everything you do and make sure there is a focus on gratitude. Are you keeping up the practice of journaling your daily gratitude? Our actions always follow our thoughts. When we build an operating system and neural pathways of gratitude, our mind automatically looks for the positive in any situation. When we fill our thoughts with fear and uncertainty, we live a life of fear and uncertainty.

Our time spent in the devotional and with our daily practice of the Lord's Prayer clears the way for authentic two-way communication with our Heavenly Father. We start with acknowledging His place in our lives, ask for forgiveness and grant it to others, rely on Him for what we need this day, and ask Him to lead us away from temptation.

Could we have a better way to start each day? We then read Scripture and reflect on it, which is His way of speaking to us.

Prayer

Thank you for this, Father. I will continue to communicate with you in daily prayer, looking up to the heavens with an alert mind, a reflective spirit, and a grateful heart. I desire a new operating system and neural pathways, and I will persevere to create them! In Jesus's name, Amen!

Daily Gratitude:

_____

_____

_____

_____

_____

_____

Reflections:

_____

_____

_____

_____

_____

_____

_____

_____

_____

Day 38

1 Peter 5:8

Stay alert! Watch out for your great enemy, the devil. He prowls around like a roaring lion, looking for someone to devour.

Mindful Minute

It is always good to remember there is an enemy at work trying to derail our path to God. In the case of any life-interfering behavior that has created sin in us, it might be "Just this one time," "I need to do this," or "I can't stop this." There are lots of stories and lots of deception about why we may miss what we once believed was our only source of comfort to fill an emotional void. There is often a deceptive romanticism about the memory of it. Remember the times prior to you starting this program when you said, "Just this once…" How did that work out?

There have been many before you who have fallen for the lie, only to re-engage an old habit that turned your attention away from God *again*. Before we get serious about doing something different, we experience many of these *do-overs* in our lives, only to start the cycle all over again. There have also been many before you who *succeeded* in conquering the temptation. They provide inspiration to us, proving it is possible to walk this path.

Let us take the wisdom of our mighty God, the wisdom and experience of our past, and the inspiration of those who walked before us in conquering the great enemy. Stay alert!

Prayer

Thank you for this, Father. I need to be reminded each day of the temptations presented to me by the devil. He is devious and cunning in his ways, looking for his prey like a lion. I will focus on you this day and stay alert! In Jesus's name I pray. Amen.

Daily Gratitude:

_____

_____

_____

_____

_____

_____

Reflections:

_____

_____

_____

_____

_____

_____

_____

_____

_____

Day 39

Psalm 51:10 (NIV)

Create in me a pure heart, O God, and renew a steadfast spirit within me.

Mindful Minute

To remain steadfast, it is important to have something to look forward to. You have many days under your belt at this point, and you might have tried some new things to fit into your new life, such as your daily habit of gratitude. Is there something you have felt called to do but have been putting it off? Through this daily process of focus on His Word, has the Holy Spirit been bringing anything to mind that should be a part of your goals? Trust in His voice. You are most likely more rested each day because of reduced anxiety which may even lead to better sleep. You most certainly have additional time on your hands because you are not participating in your old habit and are not obsessing over how you will control it every day.

To create a spirit of endurance, you must feel good about the race you are running. At the end of these twelve weeks, it will be important to reflect on not only what was given up, but it must be weighed against what you have gained.

If there is something you feel called to do and it seems too large right now, choose something that leads you in the right direction that is small, measurable, and achievable. His focus for you could be as simple as spending time with someone or just listening to an audio book. Start walking in faith and trusting yourself when you feel Spirit-led.

Prayer

Thank you, Father, for the ability to start fresh each morning and praise you and ask you to clear my mind to focus on you. You have wiped the slate clean for me, and I can take full advantage of that by hearing your voice and choosing to follow my path accordingly. Thank you, Jesus. Amen.

Daily Gratitude:

_____

_____

_____

_____

_____

_____

Reflections:

_____

_____

_____

_____

_____

_____

_____

_____

Day 40

Matthew 22:36-40

"Teacher, which is the most important commandment in the law of Moses?" Jesus replied, "'You must love the Lord your God with all your heart, all your soul, and all your mind. This is the first and greatest commandment. A second is equally important: 'Love your neighbor as yourself.' The entire law and all the demands of the prophets are based on these two commandments."

Mindful Minute

This verse is often used to communicate how important it is to love others; however, there are a couple of concepts to consider before we can genuinely love others with open hearts. First, we are instructed to love God with all our hearts. When we do, we learn the depth and breadth of the sacrifice Jesus made so we can be forgiven and forgive ourselves. It bears repeating: When we can forgive ourselves, we can move forward and look forward to a different hope.

People see the light inside of us when we are unencumbered by our past lives. Think about the most inspiring stories you have ever heard. They most assuredly are a "rags to riches" type of story. They describe how someone overcame adversity and went on to persevere despite circumstances and ultimately claimed victory over their adversity. Their unfiltered stories of overcoming inspire others.

We have an opportunity to love and become a more authentic source of love and inspiration to others if we first learn to love ourselves.

Prayer

Thank you, Father, for this reminder, and thank you, Jesus, for your sacrifice. You love me unconditionally, and I must learn to love and see myself the same way you do. When I can do this, I can make my daily choices more wisely with love and consideration for myself. I desire to claim victory over this and become a source of inspiration to others. I offer this prayer with a grateful heart. Amen.

Daily Gratitude:

_____

_____

_____

_____

_____

_____

_____

Reflections:

_____

_____

_____

_____

_____

_____

_____

_____

_____

_____

Day 41

Galatians 5:1 (NIV)

It is for freedom that Christ has set us free. Stand firm, then, and do not let yourselves be burdened again by a yoke of slavery.

Mindful Minute

Today we remember we are in a race for freedom from the psychological slavery of our life-interfering behavior. We have been blessed by His Word, which is His instruction book on how to stay the course. Let us stand firm on our faith in Jesus and the promises He has set forth for us. We must put on the armor of God, stay on the straight path, and forgive ourselves because Christ has already paid the price.

We can move forward with confidence in our choice because we understand the depth of His love for us and see ourselves as God does (as lovable). Always be prepared for adversity and stand firm. These are the new habits we are instilling through daily practices on this journey. Standing firm produces endurance, and endurance produces character, the kind of character that reflects God's nature, along with new and wonderful habits.

There is abundant science behind this godly wisdom that says the physical structure of the brain changes when we learn to face life's challenges in a positive rather than negative mindset. Healing becomes possible when we persevere.

Prayer

Father, I stand here in awe today, realizing how powerful this gift of freedom truly is. You have given us the power to choose and the freedom to do it as well. I want to choose wisely this day a path that allows me to be unencumbered by the things of the world. I choose to hope despite circumstances. I want to be open to all the possibilities You have promised me when I follow you. I want a renewed mind. In Jesus's mighty name I pray. Amen.

Daily Gratitude:

_____

_____

_____

_____

_____

_____

Reflections:

_____

_____

_____

_____

_____

_____

_____

_____

_____

Day 42

1 Peter 1:6-7

So be truly glad. There is wonderful joy ahead, even though you must endure many trials for a little while. These trials will show that your faith is genuine. It is being tested as fire tests and purifies gold—though your faith is far more precious than mere gold. So when your faith remains strong through many trials, it will bring you much praise and glory and honor on the day when Jesus Christ is revealed to the whole world.

Mindful Minute

This is the third verse used so far from 1 Peter during this twelve-week trek. Peter wrote his letter for the purpose of encouraging Christians to continue their faithful journeys despite persecution. The culture then was one where Christians were scorned, mocked, and criticized for their beliefs.

We can feel like "outsiders" in a world where certain behaviors are widely accepted and sometimes even celebrated. We now understand that many of those celebrated worldly behaviors often lead to disconnection and sin. It can be far more counter-cultural to care for our bodies and minds, have clarity in our relationships, or live a life that reflects internal joy without needing a diversion that got us trapped in sin.

We are reminded here once again that our perseverance will be tested, and we can be assured our transformation through our various trials will *bring praise and glory that is revealed to the whole world.* In other words, as you succeed in this path, you will be an inspiration to others.

Prayer

Father, I do rejoice as I pass through various trials, for I know I will find a peace and joy that surpasses all understanding, and it will ultimately be a reflection of you. Thank you, Jesus. Amen.

Daily Gratitude:

_____

_____

_____

_____

_____

_____

Reflections:

_____

_____

_____

_____

_____

_____

_____

_____

Week 7: Days 43-49

Day 43

Isaiah 41:10

Don't be afraid, for I am with you. Don't be discouraged, for I am your God. I will strengthen you and help you. I will hold you up with my victorious right hand.

Mindful Minute

This is a powerful verse to live by. Despite its applicability in so many areas of our daily lives, its wisdom here can be found and applied to those situations where we may come face to face with an event or situation or person where we feel our ability to navigate our forward path may be compromised.

There are so many events in life that cause us anxiety, sadness, or the feeling of despair. Those feelings can lead us to engage in something that we believe will give us relief from those stressors. We are challenging ourselves here because we know that's a lie. We can remind ourselves not to be afraid. We can remind ourselves not to be discouraged. We can tell ourselves we "get to" succeed in this situation. We get to have control over our thoughts related to this habit instead of allowing it to have control over us.

Staying on this path allows God's plan for us to unfold. Each time we face a challenging situation and succeed, we are strengthening new habits and neural pathways. God is with us, always.

Prayer

Father, today I am grateful because I know I am loved and cared for. When I don't feel strong enough to endure a trial, I can feel you holding me up. I can have hope in a future that always has you in it. This fact allows me to always choose gratitude, despite circumstances. In Jesus' mighty name. Amen.

Daily Gratitude:

_____

_____

_____

_____

_____

Reflections:

_____

_____

_____

_____

_____

_____

_____

Day 44

Hebrews 11:1

Faith shows the reality of what we hope for; it is the evidence of things we cannot see.

Mindful Minute

As we walk this path day by day and meditate on God's Word, our faith and relationship with Him deepen. Our relationship and bond become stronger such that we develop a love that endures, and we trust in His promise for us. The closing line of the Lord's Prayer reminds us of what we believe but cannot see: "For yours is the kingdom and the power and the glory forever." He is in charge. He has won the battle. He has a plan, the story is written, and we will have a place in His house for eternity. His promise for us on earth also includes plans for us to prosper (Jeremiah 29:11), and while we might not yet see or understand what the plan is, we can continue to walk this path and have the same faith. Our faith and relationship with Him do indeed become the evidence for things we cannot see.

As you reflect daily through this journey, don't forget to document the evidence that is showing up as you continue this path with Him. It will ultimately be the *evidence of things we cannot see.*

Prayer

Father, today I choose to have faith in what I will become when I choose to live a life free from the toxic and life-interfering behaviors that tempt me. Thank you, Jesus. I place my trust in you today and every day. Amen.

Daily Gratitude:

_____

_____

_____

_____

_____

_____

Reflections:

_____

_____

_____

_____

_____

_____

_____

_____

_____

Day 45

1 Thessalonians 5:14-22

Brothers and sisters, we urge you to warn those who are lazy. Encourage those who are timid. Take tender care of those who are weak. Be patient with everyone. See that no one pays back evil for evil but always try to do good to each other and to all people. Always be joyful. Never stop praying. Be thankful in all circumstances, for this is God's will for you who belong to Christ Jesus. Do not stifle the Holy Spirit. Do not scoff at prophecies, but test everything that is said. Hold on to what is good. Stay away from every kind of evil.

Mindful Minute

Chapter 5 of 1 Thessalonians discusses the day of the Lord's second coming. Paul writes not only about the second coming but also lets us know how we should be living our lives in preparation for His arrival. As we reflect on the successes in our walk to change this neurological habit thus far, we have been given the gift of time today to examine just how many things in our life have become available to us by refraining from a behavior that has caused so much havoc.

Are you more confident? Do you have less anxiety? Is your mood better? Are you getting more done? Are you better able to think through the problems life has thrown at you? Are your relationships better? If you are honest with yourself, the hours stolen from you by engaging in this habit prohibited you from fully participating in all that is asked of you in anticipation of His second coming. These verses show this to be true.

Prayer

Father, I want to live life to the fullest. I want to live a life full of joy that allows your light to reflect through me. I understand that to do all of this, I must have a clear mind and conscience. Today I will remember to hold on to what is good. Thank you for the gift of forgiveness that allows me to start fresh each day and look forward with hope. In Jesus' name. Amen.

Daily Gratitude:

_____

_____

_____

_____

_____

_____

Reflections:

_____

_____

_____

_____

_____

_____

_____

_____

Day 46

James 1:13-16

And remember, when you are being tempted, do not say, "God is tempting me." God is never tempted to do wrong, and he never tempts anyone else. Temptation comes from our own desires, which entice us and drag us away. These desires give birth to sinful actions. And when sin is allowed to grow, it gives birth to death. So don't be misled, my dear brothers and sisters.

Mindful Minute

The temptation to engage in a toxic behavior is rooted in repeated actions from the past, which created a habit loop in our unconscious mind. Our own actions instilled the deeply rooted neurological pathway, and yet our own new actions can also create new pathways! Remember, temptation will present itself, sometimes at very inopportune moments. It is in those moments when we have a choice. The choice we make will depend on taking a longer view beyond the present moment.

On the other side of twelve weeks, and beyond, who do we want to see when we look in the mirror? Focus on the promises of our loving God, for He only desires the best life for us. When the long view is in play, we are equipped to handle temptation. When we begin to waver and think about satisfying the flesh, be reminded of the endgame, and the guilt and shame that will follow poor choices.

Play the movie through to the end and be reminded about the definition of insanity, which is doing the same thing over and over but expecting different results. God has a plan for you that is far greater than any temptation in the moment. Don't be misled!

Prayer

Father, let me remember this day and every day how my own unhealthy desires give birth to sin. When I sin, I bring to myself guilt and shame. Guilt and shame kill my joyful spirit. I choose "light" today. I choose to remain free from psychological slavery. I choose joy in the comfort of your unconditional love. I choose the long view. In Jesus' name. Amen.

Daily Gratitude:

Reflections:

Day 47

Philippians 3:13

No, dear brothers and sisters, I have not achieved it, but I focus on this one thing: Forgetting the past and looking forward to what lies ahead.

Mindful Minute

We are all marked in our lives by events of the past. Our experiences create a story for each of us that starts to develop into a personality and a way of thinking. This verse starts with a powerful acknowledgment that we cannot always perfectly achieve forgetting our past, and yet we can recognize when we are living in it and shift our focus forward to what is possible.

A world where we can accept the past for what it is, forgive others, and forgive ourselves allows the beautiful being God created in us to emerge and operate, looking forward to seeing the possibilities of a better life. Living in the past prohibits us from seeing a different future. What part of your past do you need to be mindful of and let go? You may not achieve it (forgetting the past), and yet you will be able to identify it when it comes up, label it as "the past," and dismiss it to give you the ability to look forward.

Prayer

Father, you have cleared a path for me that is unencumbered by every sin of my own and of others towards me. Forgiveness is available to all who ask, and the burden of those who sin against us must not be placed within ourselves. I now understand why wiping the slate clean is needed to be all that you see in me. When the past comes up, I will label it as such and look instead to the future possibilities. Thank you, Jesus. Amen.

Daily Gratitude:

Reflections:

Day 48

Hebrews 10:11-18

Under the old covenant, the priest stands and ministers before the altar day after day, offering the same sacrifices again and again, which can never take away sins. But our High Priest offered himself to God as a single sacrifice for sins, good for all time... For by that one offering he forever made perfect those who are being made holy... Then he says, "I will never again remember their sins and lawless deeds." And when sins have been forgiven, there is no need to offer any more sacrifices.

Mindful Minute

These verses are a reminder of how the old system of sacrifice was completely and forever replaced by the sacrifice made by Jesus on the cross. The critical point here is that we do not have to repeatedly repent for past sins. Once forgiveness is asked for, it is forever and permanently granted. The word "perfect" is used because it means complete and fulfilled without the need for anything further to be done. We are restored in His eyes to the state *prior* to the sin.

The practical resistance for many in accomplishing this for themselves lies in restoring themselves to the state of being prior to the sin. Can you imagine the possibilities of truly accepting ourselves as perfect and complete and restored because of His sacrifice? It would mean we would be free to live and operate in a way where we could realize the full potential of our gifts. Are there sins in your past you would like to erase? How would you be free to operate if you could acknowledge that God has wiped the slate clean to a time prior to the sin?

This is the place in which you can realize your greatest God-given potential and give up the distraction of thoughts and doubts caused by sin.

Prayer

Father, I am forgiven. I desire the freedom to "be" and operate in a world where I see myself unencumbered by the sin of my past. I want to look forward and continue my walk so I can use the gifts you have given me to be a light in this world and make a difference through your Holy Spirit in the lives of the people with whom I come into contact. Thank you, Jesus. Amen.

Daily Gratitude:

_____

_____

_____

_____

_____

_____

_____

Reflections:

_____

_____

_____

_____

_____

_____

_____

_____

_____

_____

Day 49

Ephesians 4:30-32

And do not bring sorrow to God's Holy Spirit by the way you live. Remember, he has identified you as his own, guaranteeing that you will be saved on the day of redemption. Get rid of all bitterness, rage, anger, harsh words, and slander, as well as all types of evil behavior. Instead, be kind to each other, tenderhearted, forgiving one another, just as God through Christ has forgiven you.

Mindful Minute

Yesterday, we reflected on what "forgiveness of self" looks like. God's view of wiping the slate clean is like turning back the clock to the moment before the sin occurred. It is fully forgiven and forgotten by our Heavenly Father. That doesn't mean He has amnesia. It means He chooses not to hold it against us *ever again*.

God also calls us to forgive others, not only as an act of obedience but to free ourselves from the burden of grudges and the stress they create in our bodies. Today's verses reflect God's sorrow over the way we sometimes choose to live.

The way we choose to live is almost always dictated by the culmination of a series of events, whether good or evil. It is the felt experience resulting from sin and evil that creates anger, bitterness, and rage within us. It is here where we get to choose to forgive, just as God has forgiven us.

What would our choices and behaviors look like if we were able to remove the bitterness inside us that was created by an unforgiving heart?

Prayer

Father, I am overwhelmed by the idea that I can turn back the clock to a time before sin occurred in my life, both related to my sin and the sin of others, for the purpose of experiencing your forgiveness. My yoke is truly easy and light when I choose to follow you. Thank you, Jesus, for your sacrifice so I can live freely, no longer weighed down by the sins of the past. Amen.

Daily Gratitude:

_____

_____

_____

_____

_____

_____

Reflections:

_____

_____

_____

_____

_____

_____

_____

_____

_____

Week 8: Days 50–56

Day 50

James 1:22-24

But don't just listen to God's word. You must do what it says. Otherwise, you are only fooling yourselves. For if you listen to the word and don't obey, it is like glancing at your face in a mirror. You see yourself, walk away, and forget what you look like.

Mindful Minute

How many of us have experienced going to church on a Sunday and feeling "renewed" at the possibility of a changed heart and attitude only to walk out of the church and just hours later lose that sense of purpose? This is the very reason we are creating new neural habits during this twelve-week period of daily devotional focus, practice, and prayer. By creating a habit of studying His word, we will be less likely to forget it during our daily walk. It is the very reason why God asks us to "meditate on His word" in Joshua:

> This Book of the Law shall not depart from your mouth, but you shall meditate on it day and night, so that you may be careful to do according to all that is written in it. For then you will make your way prosperous, and then you will have good success (Joshua 1:8, ESV).

God's promises are true. The new daily practice we are engaging in will give us the ability to create the life we so desperately desire. We are creating a new identity in Christ. Deviation from His Word causes us to forget who we are and what we were created to be.

Prayer

Father, sometimes it is so much easier to know what to do than it is to put it into practice. I need to remind myself today and every day that choosing what is good will yield the results I desire. You always know what is best for me, and you love me enough to give me this freedom of choice. I no longer want to be a victim of desires I know do not serve me or you. Thank you, Jesus. Amen.

Daily Gratitude:

_____

_____

_____

_____

_____

_____

Reflections:

_____

_____

_____

_____

_____

_____

_____

_____

Day 51

Psalm 84:11

For the Lord God is our sun and shield. He gives us grace and glory. The Lord will withhold no good thing from those who do what is right.

Mindful Minute

We should be experiencing more freedom in our walk as we continue to make choices that are in line with our Heavenly Father's wisdom. When we spend time in the Word of God, we come to understand that He is the source of all light in the world. It is impossible for darkness to overcome the light. Light exposes and obliterates darkness. Just open a closet door and turn the light on to test the theory. When Jesus was born, we are told that the wise men followed a star to lead them to the Savior. Our verse today reminds us that the Lord God is a light for us that will provide the path to find Him every moment of every day. We want to continue to walk toward that light.

We are also told that God is our shield. By choosing the path He has set out for us, the light will shield us from the darkness and all the consequences that come about when we stray from the path of light. This verse tells us that He will not withhold from those who choose His path. What a comforting thought and promise. Believe in His promises.

Prayer

Heavenly Father, I want to continue this path with your light as my North Star, giving me the wisdom and direction I need to choose you. I desire to continue this path and walk uprightly so that I may experience the good things you promise. Thank you, Jesus. In your mighty name I pray. Amen.

Daily Gratitude:

_____

_____

_____

_____

_____

_____

Reflections:

_____

_____

_____

_____

_____

_____

_____

_____

_____

Day 52

1 Corinthians 10:23-24

You say, "I am allowed to do anything"—but not everything is good for you. You say, "I am allowed to do anything"—but not everything is beneficial. Don't be concerned for your own good but for the good of others.

Mindful Minute

When we are truly rooted in the reality that *"this world"* is the domain of *"the ruler of the kingdom of the air"* (Ephesians 2:2, NIV), we begin to see more clearly that what is deemed acceptable and in many cases legal does not necessarily benefit us or our bodies. Whether it's online gaming, gambling, pornography, shopping, overeating, or other behaviors related to food, we must recognize that while these things are legal and may provide brief moments of enjoyment, they often come at a cost.

Upon closer examination of each choice, we begin to see that legality does not equal health. And if it is not healthy, it will not bring healing, peace, or meaningful joy. In fact, many of these behaviors can and often do lead to greater anxiety, declining health, and a deeper sense of disconnection from others and, most importantly, from our Creator because of the priority these behaviors begin to take in our lives.

This verse provides us with a deeper perspective about how to examine our choices in things that are freely acceptable in the world around us, yet truly harmful to our overall wellbeing. This verse is about being concerned about what is good for others. Our choices provide inspiration, light, and love to others.

When we abstain from things that are overall toxic to our well-being, we are giving permission for others to do the same. Getting rid of our toxic habit will ultimately also allow the Holy Spirit to shine in our being, thereby providing a light to others.

Prayer

Father, I recognize the psychological state of slavery I was in when I formed habits with things that are of this world and lawful yet harmful to my personal well-being and spiritual growth. I am beginning to enjoy the freedom of operating in this world where I am not succumbing to those legal things that create bondage, and I see the path forward to being an inspiration for others. I choose freedom in you so all may see the joy it brings. In Jesus' name. Amen.

Daily Gratitude:

_____

_____

_____

_____

_____

_____

Reflections:

_____

_____

_____

_____

_____

_____

_____

_____

_____

Day 53

Luke 6:48-49

It is like a person building a house who digs deep and lays the foundation on solid rock. When the floodwaters rise and break against that house, it stands firm because it is well-built. But anyone who hears and doesn't obey is like a person who builds a house right on the ground, without a foundation. When the floods sweep down against that house, it will collapse into a heap of ruins.

Mindful Minute

Spending daily time with God in this devotional is building a solid foundation in gratitude, prayer, and meditation on His Word. When doing so, we are better able to combat the enemy's strategies moving forward. When the floodwaters and crashing waves of our life break against the foundation of truth we are building, our new ways of thinking will guard us against the pounding effect of those waves of emotions.

Because of gratitude, we will be able to look at the situation with the glass half full instead of half empty. Because of our prayers, we will be reminded that He is with us in any battle we are faced with, and we don't need to do it alone. Because of our meditation on His word, we will be reminded of His truth and be prepared to capture any thought that is directed to us that represents a false narrative.

We can redirect that thought and make it obedient to Christ (2 Corinthians 10:5). And because we acknowledge how much He loves us, we are reminded that acting on temptation is an act of self-hatred. As this verse tells us, it will collapse us back into the heap of ruins we started from.

Prayer

Thank you, Father, for your Word that gives us a solid foundation from which to withstand the storms that come about in our lives. I desire to continue this foundation building so that the waves cannot affect the fortress that has been built within me. I do not want to return to the ruins that got me to this place, and I will continue to practice being in relationship with you moving forward. Thank you, Jesus. Amen.

Daily Gratitude:

_____

_____

_____

_____

_____

_____

Reflections:

_____

_____

_____

_____

_____

_____

_____

_____

_____

Day 54

Hebrews 8:12

And I will forgive their wickedness, and I will never again remember their sins.

Mindful Minute

The primary focus of Hebrews Chapter 8 is on the new covenant that has been offered by the sacrifice of Jesus on the cross. In this Chapter, the writer of Hebrews quotes prophecy in Jeremiah and talks of a time when God will put the law in people's minds and *write it on their hearts*. This is a beautiful picture of how we come to a place where we recognize sin and come to God with a repentant heart. It is then that we can experience the promise of Him remembering our sin no more. This is not about amnesia. History stays intact. Instead, it's about understanding that Jesus did all of the work to restore our relationship with our Heavenly Father so that we can focus on a better plan for us in the future.

We are free to move forward to explore our potential instead of being tied to our past with a ball and chain. We no longer need to get stuck in mistakes of our past because it creates massive roadblocks to achieving everything that is conceivable in the future.

The practice of forgiving yourself is critical to moving forward with a better plan. Many times we can intellectually understand this but not "feel" forgiven. Our feelings do not always represent truth, especially as it relates to this subject matter. Sometimes, when we struggle with forgiveness, we just need to learn to *agree with* God. Otherwise, we are thinking we know better than Him, and clearly, we do not.

Prayer

Thank you, Father, for reminding me this day that I can let go of the past and choose to look forward. I will meditate on your Word as I find the peace within that surpasses any worldly understanding. I know I have been forgiven, and I recognize how releasing what is behind is critical for your promised rewards in the future. Thank you, Jesus, for dying on the cross and relieving me of this burden called sin. Amen.

Daily Gratitude:

_____

_____

_____

_____

_____

_____

Reflections:

_____

_____

_____

_____

_____

_____

_____

_____

_____

Day 55

1 John 4:18

Such love has no fear, because perfect love expels all fear. If we are afraid, it is for fear of punishment, and this shows that we have not fully experienced his perfect love.

Mindful Minute

Thought to be written by John the apostle, 1 John displays simplicity in its message through its "either/or" approach. The comparison here is fear versus love. The phrase "Fear not" is mentioned in the Bible hundreds of times. Given the repetitive nature of these particular words through the entirety of Scripture, it is worth our time, energy, and focus to examine them further.

We go through life with unending worldly fears: fear of failing, fear of being judged, fear of looking bad, fear of not fitting in, fear of being lonely, fear of spiders or heights—the list is endless. Biological fear was meant for protection against physical danger, and there is an appropriate biological reaction available to us when in real physical danger. When we are not in physical danger, fear is futile, and it is a disempowering felt experience. Fear detracts from our decisions and reactions toward others.

Examine your fears and see if they come from a place of legitimate danger or whether they are the result of an earthly anxiety you could replace with love of self and love of others.

Prayer

Father, I want to choose my actions out of love and not out of fear. I want to love myself unconditionally so I can love others in the same manner. I will recognize and acknowledge when others act out of fear as well. I want to live confidently in my decisions and feel empowered to influence others by my own choices that are directed by love, not fear. In Jesus' name. Amen.

Daily Gratitude:

_____

_____

_____

_____

_____

_____

Reflections:

_____

_____

_____

_____

_____

_____

_____

_____

_____

Day 56

Daniel 10:19

"Don't be afraid," he said, "for you are very precious to God. Peace! Be encouraged! Be strong!" As he spoke these words to me, I suddenly felt stronger and said to him, "Please speak to me, my lord, for you have strengthened me."

Mindful Minute

In these verses, Daniel is having a vision of something he is frightened about when the pre-incarnate Jesus appears to him and speaks these words. This is a story from the Old Testament. Today, we now have the risen Jesus in action through the Holy Spirit within us. The message then (over 2,000 years ago) is the same as it is today. When we put our trust in Jesus, the things that cause us fear will dissipate. When we examine fear, whether it is real (true danger) or imagined (perceived danger), we must find a way to have peace in knowing the story has already been written.

God is in control. Being encouraged and being strong is the message. Strength, courage, and the elimination of fear equal transformation!

Prayer

Father, I will put one foot in front of the other. I will run the race with perseverance because I know what you have promised me is peace. I want peace in my life, Father. I look forward to what the future holds and your promises for me as I continue to put my trust in you. Thank you, Jesus, for your message to me this day. I am precious. Amen.

Daily Gratitude:

_____

_____

_____

_____

_____

_____

Reflections:

_____

_____

_____

_____

_____

_____

_____

_____

_____

Week 9: Days 57-63

Day 57

Luke 6:43-45

A good tree can't produce bad fruit, and a bad tree can't produce good fruit. A tree is identified by its fruit. Figs are never gathered from thorn bushes, and grapes are not picked from bramble bushes. A good person produces good things from the treasury of a good heart, and an evil person produces evil things from the treasury of an evil heart. What you say flows from what is in your heart.

Mindful Minute

God created us in His image, beautiful beings who were designed to be good. But sin marred the image of God in us. Yet God provided Jesus to restore His image within us! And through Jesus we can be restored to God's original design, beautiful people who bear the image of God and who share God's beauty with others. When we can accept this, we can then see the possibilities of using our God-given gifts to produce fruit. Satan is the prince of the power of the air, and unfortunately, sin abounds on this earth as the enemy deceives many into sinful actions (Ephesians 2:2).

Often, the events of the past (usually founded in sin) define stories in our heads that prohibit us from living in the freedom of what is possible. We develop fears because of those stories and hold on to them so tightly that we convince ourselves what we dream is simply not possible anymore. Has your habit stood in the way of you realizing something you want to achieve, even if it is simply *peace*? Is there a gift you are not using because of some story that creates fear in you?

Look up, take a chance, and stretch into the discomfort to see something different. The same actions will produce the same results. What fruit is possible because of your God-given gifts?

Prayer

Father, thank you for providing the ultimate sacrifice in Jesus so my slate can be wiped clean each day I live on this earth. My habits of the past have greatly affected my abilities to produce all the good fruit that is possible. Thank you for loving me just the way I am today. I am eternally grateful. My desire in return is to produce much good fruit. In Jesus' mighty name. Amen.

Daily Gratitude:

_____

_____

_____

_____

_____

_____

Reflections:

_____

_____

_____

_____

_____

_____

_____

_____

_____

Day 58

Proverbs 17:22

A cheerful heart is good medicine, but a broken spirit saps a person's strength.

Mindful Minute

Science again and again confirms what God has tried to communicate to us for thousands of years. Gratitude for all that is good creates psychological well-being, and psychological well-being creates good physical health. Many of the versions of this verse translate "saps a person's strength" as "drying up of the bones." Regardless of which translation you like, we understand both scientifically and biblically that looking at the glass as half-full instead of half-empty is powerful for our emotional and physical well-being. We know we have been robbed of a cheerful heart when our habit gained control of us. Now we have chosen to be on this journey of transformation.

Can you identify where there might still be a broken spirit within you? Continue to search. Continue to focus on things around you that are good. Continue to forgive, both yourself and others.

Prayer

Father, thank you for your Word this day. I desire a cheerful heart. I want a clear conscience as I move forward in this journey so I can feel and express authentic joy. "Search me, God, and know my heart; test me and know my anxious thoughts. See if there is any offensive way in me and lead me in the way everlasting," Psalm 139:23–24, (NIV). Thank you, Jesus, for your sacrifice on the cross. I desire to understand what it means to wipe the slate clean. Amen.

Daily Gratitude:

_____

_____

_____

_____

_____

_____

Reflections:

_____

_____

_____

_____

_____

_____

_____

_____

_____

Day 59

Proverbs 10:9

People with integrity walk safely, but those who follow crooked paths will
be exposed.

Mindful Minute

After weeks of spending time in the devotional, we're beginning to see real change in
our habits. We're also starting to feel more grounded and secure in our daily choices.
Temptation may still show up at our doorstep, but with each passing challenge, our
neural pathways grow stronger.

The word "integrity" has two meanings. The first deals with being honest and having
strong moral principles, and the second meaning deals with a sense of completeness. In this journey, the aspect of integrity most important to focus on here is keeping the promises you've made to yourself. It is much easier to have integrity in our
word with others than it is with ourselves.

The longer you stay the course, the stronger your neural pathways get and the more
complete you feel. This feeling of completeness allows the Holy Spirit to navigate
within as you discover the beauty of the person you were created to be.

There is no hiding on the crooked path. All (God, self, and others) eventually find
out when integrity is breached because the results of it are evident in our being.

Prayer

Father, thank you for your reminder today of how integrity to me matters. I desire
completeness of being so I may experience the power of who you created me to
be. Thank you, Jesus, for your sacrifice so I can stop the past from interfering with
what's possible for my future. Amen.

Daily Gratitude:

_____

_____

_____

_____

_____

_____

Reflections:

_____

_____

_____

_____

_____

_____

_____

_____

_____

Day 60

Psalm 41:11-12

By this I know that you delight in me: my enemy will not shout in triumph over me. But you have upheld me because of my integrity and set me in your presence forever.

Mindful Minute

The discussion yesterday was one of having integrity with yourself. The root Hebrew word here for integrity does, in fact, mean *completeness*. God delights in us when we have completeness and integrity with self. We can triumph over our enemies because of the light of the Holy Spirit. The only possible way to defeat darkness is with light. We cannot battle darkness. It takes too much of our energy to go into battle, but darkness simply disappears in the light. Access to the Holy Spirit's brightness becomes much easier when we "stay the path," put on the armor of God, and have integrity with our word to ourselves.

The system in place through the sacrifice of Jesus allows us to put any sins of the past away. It is through remembrance of this that we can move forward with confidence.

Prayer

Father, the enemy is always near, but I desire triumph. I desire light. I desire integrity with myself and with others. Thank you, Jesus, for your sacrifice that allows me to continue to look forward and not back. Amen.

Daily Gratitude:

_____

_____

_____

_____

_____

_____

Reflections:

_____

_____

_____

_____

_____

_____

_____

_____

_____

Day 61

Hebrews 13:18

Pray for us, for our conscience is clear and we want to live honorably in everything we do.

Mindful Minute

At this point in your twelve-week journey, your conscience is most likely quite clear regarding the integrity you've demonstrated in abstaining from a behavior that once interfered with your life. Take a moment to remind yourself of the personal victories you've experienced during this time. Do not take for granted the wins that have come from your hard work and commitment to a straighter path.

How has your productivity improved? Has your self-confidence grown as you navigate more confidently around this toxic habit? How have your relationships improved? How has your daily focus on gratitude and God shaped your life?

Taking a moment to reflect on the positive impact of removing this habit will strengthen your resolve and help you move forward with a clear conscience. Continue your walk with humility, which requires prayer. Honor will follow.

Prayer

Father, how freeing it is to have a clear conscience from this thing that kept me in psychological slavery. I desire to continue this path each day as I experience the joy in your promises. This freedom helps me to make other decisions to act honorably and gives me the confidence to move boldly through this world. I choose this clear conscience because it shows light and hope for others. Thank you, Jesus. Amen.

Daily Gratitude:

_____

_____

_____

_____

_____

_____

Reflections:

_____

_____

_____

_____

_____

_____

_____

_____

_____

Day 62

Psalm 37:1-6

Don't worry about the wicked or envy those who do wrong. For like grass, they soon fade away. Like spring flowers, they soon wither. Trust in the Lord and do good. Then you will live safely in the land and prosper. Take delight in the Lord, and he will give you your heart's desires. Commit everything you do to the Lord. Trust him, and he will help you. He will make your innocence radiate like the dawn, and the justice of your cause will shine like the noonday sun.

Mindful Minute

As you gain more confidence in your journey, it is natural to start minimizing the effects your habit previously had on you. We usually remember harm inflicted on us by others but easily develop amnesia for hurtful consequences we inflict on ourselves. You will most likely begin to think that what you were doing wasn't really *that* bad. Others do it and might manage it just fine. Maybe I can just do this occasionally or mistakenly believe that life is no longer fun if I don't continue to engage in it. Know that these are deceptive ways of the enemy to get you back into the habit loop that has been well-ingrained in your mind.

This verse encourages us to trust in God and continue the journey. Stay the course to receive the "desires of your heart," because those desires may not even be evident to you today as your habit dulled your senses about what was possible. Begin writing down what the "unencumbered" you looks and feels like. Listen to the voice of the Holy Spirit because the voice is getting louder, and your ability to radiate His light to others will be evident.

Think back about what you longed for prior to committing to this journey. Take some time to assess where you are in comparison to what your heart's desire was in relieving you from this habit that was enslaving you.

Prayer

Father, I want to continue this path I have begun. I am beginning to see the light get brighter and brighter in front of me. I am grateful for the release of these chains that bound me. I will continue this path and not be envious of those around me because I realize this could cause me to stumble. I will focus on all that I have been given so far on this journey. Thank you, Jesus! Amen.

Daily Gratitude:

_____

_____

_____

_____

_____

_____

Reflections:

_____

_____

_____

_____

_____

_____

_____

_____

_____

Day 63

Philippians 4:8

And now, dear brothers and sisters, one final thing. Fix your thoughts on what is true, and honorable, and right, and pure, and lovely, and admirable. Think about things that are excellent and worthy of praise.

Mindful Minute

It is always a wonderful reminder that when trials of any kind come, fixing our thoughts on what is true, honorable, and right will help us get through. When it comes to those life-interfering behaviors that became habits, thoughts and temptations will still try to creep into our daily lives, whispering the lie that engaging in them was truly "wonderful." We begin to romanticize the behavior and wish it could somehow be part of our lives again. Now that you're feeling more confident living without that destructive habit, you might be tempted to believe the lie that "just once" won't hurt.

This is the moment when you *must* focus on what is true and pure, what is right and admirable. With each trigger we push aside, we strengthen the neural pathway for achievement and success in this endeavor. The tempting thoughts will dissipate, getting weaker and weaker over time. Keep up with the daily gratitude list. It helps us focus on things that are positive and true in our lives.

Prayer

Yes, Father, living a life of gratitude makes all the difference in the world. I will wake up each day committed to thinking of what is good in what I see around me. Focusing on these things allows me to put into perspective all those things that may cause me to stumble. I am committed to living a life of gratitude. Thank you, Jesus. Amen.

Daily Gratitude:

_____

_____

_____

_____

_____

_____

_____

Reflections:

_____

_____

_____

_____

_____

_____

_____

_____

_____

_____

Week 10: Days 64-70

Day 64

Proverbs 3:1-2

My child, never forget the things I have taught you. Store my commands in your heart. If you do this, you will live many years, and your life will be satisfying.

Mindful Minute

There is a reason the Jews were asked to memorize the Scriptures. It is so they would never forget the words and wisdom of the Lord. It is easy sometimes to forget (or choose to forget) the admonitions of Scripture. Many people, both believers and non-believers, have confidence in the wisdom provided throughout Scripture, yet when push comes to shove, and people need to align their behavior in accordance with biblical wisdom, they revert to believing that the Bible's Scripture consists of just a bunch of rules to put us under submission. When examined closely, however, we can see it is loving guidance meant for us to lead a long life full of abundance and filled with the Holy Spirit.

Take a moment on this day to remember the various benefits you have experienced because you have refrained from engaging in whatever your life-interfering behavior was. How many other benefits do you have access to because of taking away this habit? We have choices moving forward, but this Scripture reminds us to "never forget."

Prayer

Yes, Father, I will meditate daily on your Word, with gratitude. I desire the kind of peace and prosperity only you can provide. Meditation, prayer, and gratitude produce peace and prosperity. Thank you, Jesus. Amen.

Daily Gratitude:

_____

_____

_____

_____

_____

_____

Reflections:

_____

_____

_____

_____

_____

_____

_____

_____

_____

Day 65

1 Peter 3:16

But do this in a gentle and respectful way. Keep your conscience clear. Then if people speak against you, they will be ashamed when they see what a good life you live because you belong to Christ.

Mindful Minute

This is a powerful reminder of the peace you've gained by stepping away from a behavior that once had control over your life. As you approach stressful situations that may have caused you to stumble in the past, you have now learned how to manage them with greater clarity and focus. Your responses to others are likely gentler and more respectful because you have removed a toxic habit and replaced it with a daily habit of Scripture to guide you.

Knowing there is a better plan for your life as you follow Him is a powerful motivator for the future. In this world, there will always be people who try to slander you. Your newfound gentle nature will give you the confidence to continue your walk forward in Christ. Keep your conscience clear. It is and will continue to be rewarding.

Prayer

I want my conscience to remain steadfast and clear, Father. It is with this perseverance I can stand strong and not allow the actions of others to interfere with my personal goals. When I am focused on pleasing and loving you, I know I am safe, and it gives me great peace. Thank you, Jesus. Amen.

Daily Gratitude:

_____

_____

_____

_____

_____

_____

Reflections:

_____

_____

_____

_____

_____

_____

_____

_____

Day 66

1 Timothy 1:5

The purpose of my instruction is that all believers would be filled with love that comes from a pure heart, a clear conscience, and genuine faith.

Mindful Minute

After so many days of praying, focusing, and meditating on God's word as it relates to our lives and this habit, it becomes so much clearer to us that by removing it, our hearts can love others so much more genuinely. By removing much of the anxiety in our life that was associated with our habit, we have freed our conscience and created space for the Holy Spirit. We have been forgiven, which means we can clear the way for the future.

This journey of refocus allows for more love and acceptance of self, along with love and acceptance of others. The greatest commandment from God is to "love," according to Matthew 22 (love of God, love of self, and love of others). The psychological slavery associated with our repeated sinful habit stole this extraordinary capacity to love from us. We are now able to explore it with new freedom.

Prayer

Father, it gets clearer and clearer to me each day how setting this habit aside increases my capacity to love others and myself. Without that internal judge who continues to question me, I am *free* to see more clearly and love more intensely. My love is not aimed at seeking approval. It is now authentic and in the form of a gift that never needs to be repaid. I now see more of what is possible in all my relationships and comprehend in a much deeper way the love that comes from a pure heart. Thank you, Jesus. Amen.

Daily Gratitude:

_____

_____

_____

_____

_____

_____

_____

Reflections:

_____

_____

_____

_____

_____

_____

_____

_____

_____

Day 67

2 Corinthians 4:16-18

That is why we never give up. Though our bodies are dying, our spirits are being renewed every day. For our present troubles are small and won't last very long. Yet they produce for us a glory that vastly outweighs them and will last forever! So we don't look at the troubles we can see now; rather, we fix our gaze on things that cannot be seen. For the things we see now will soon be gone, but the things we cannot see will last forever.

Mindful Minute

Just one evening of news confirms for us the evil that exists and swirls around us on a continual basis. Regardless of how many days we can have that are filled with joy, peace, and contentment, we should never forget that struggles and heartbreak can test us at any moment in our own lives. It is the practice of daily gratitude, prayer, and meditation on His Word that prepares us to "never give up." Take the time to assess how committed you are to your daily practices related to gratitude, prayer, and meditation on His Word this week.

This verse talks about keeping our gaze on the future promises of Jesus. Our purpose on this earth is to live a life filled with the Holy Spirit and hope so others can see and feel His presence. Joy, despite circumstances, is only possible when we can fix our gaze on the things that cannot be seen. While we may not be able to "see" what is in the future, we can certainly experience it through His love and His Word.

Prayer

Father, thank you for your Word today. Experiencing it daily has allowed me to understand how your instructions keep us in a state of gratitude and hope for your promise of an everlasting life with you. I can have peace that this world full of sorrow is not my final place. I want to be a light amidst sorrow, reflecting your love. I can only do so by "never giving up." Thank you, Jesus, for your sacrifice on the cross. Amen.

Daily Gratitude:

_____

_____

_____

_____

_____

_____

Reflections:

_____

_____

_____

_____

_____

_____

_____

_____

_____

Day 68

James 4:17

Remember, it is sin to know what you ought to do and then not do it.

Mindful Minute

As difficult as it might be to acknowledge this statement, there is absolute truth to it. When we accept Jesus as our Savior, we begin a journey of getting to know Him through His Word. We begin to understand how what is written in Scripture is far from being rules meant to restrict us. Holy Scripture is designed as a loving guide to help us live a life full of joy. Scripture, when read with the acceptance of the Holy Spirit, speaks to us clearly. It convicts us of the areas in our lives that are misaligned with God's best for us, and we develop a powerful thing called a conscience. It becomes easier and easier to choose the path that He has guided us to.

Hopefully, you are beginning to see there is a larger sense of confidence in your actions. There is more integrity in how you navigate your time, situations, and relationships. Knowing this Scripture makes it easier to understand how returning to that behavior represents a turning away from God's best for you. It becomes sin when, in our hearts, we know better and sense His prompting, yet still choose to ignore it. These choices may not seem outwardly harmful at first, but they can gradually interfere with our peace, clarity, and witness to others. They can dull the light of the Holy Spirit shining through us.

Yes, we will be forgiven again and again, as often as needed. He will never forsake us and will always love us unconditionally. This much is guaranteed. Though forgiveness is always available, choosing obedience spares us from unnecessary pain and draws us closer to God's best for us.

Prayer

Father, as I continue to develop new habits and leave the old ones in the past, the realization of just how deep your love is for me is overwhelming. It is easy to conceptually understand sin, but it is the ultimate gift to be able to wake up each morning and ask you to wipe the slate clean for me. As I practice and succeed in choosing the "right thing," I come to understand in such a deeply emotional way the freedom it produces, the capacity for self-love, and the motivation to be steadfast in this journey. Thank you, Jesus. Amen.

Daily Gratitude:

_____

_____

_____

_____

_____

_____

Reflections:

_____

_____

_____

_____

_____

_____

_____

_____

_____

Day 69

Titus 2:7

And you yourself must be an example to them by doing good works of every kind. Let everything you do reflect the integrity and seriousness of your teaching.

Mindful Minute

In this Scripture, Titus is being told to be an example of what he is teaching others. The reading of the whole of Chapter 2 in Titus is highly encouraged because it speaks to living in a way that honors God. It speaks to loving our spouses and children, living wisely, earning respect, and refraining from slandering (and even from heavy drinking). While we must understand that all of us fall short of the Glory of God and sin, we must also understand how a repeated behavior that is consuming our time and thoughts would interfere greatly with this admonition about being a good example to others.

So many God-fearing/loving Christians either hide in plain sight with shame or, worse yet, preach to others about right living, yet are not living rightly themselves. Little do we realize how these inconsistencies in teaching and living can have the opposite effect of what is desired in bringing people to Christ. We must, in humility, reflect the integrity and seriousness of our teachings with our behavior.

Our role on this earth is to be a light for others to follow Jesus. We do not all have to be preachers, but when we proclaim Jesus as our Savior, by default we become evangelists by our way of being and living in the world. Living a life by example is sometimes the best teaching possible in a world filled with so much suffering.

Prayer

Father, how quickly I can forget about this instruction and guidance. All eyes are upon me when I profess my love for you. This "habit" of mine has clearly impeded my ability to model good behaviors. Thank you, Jesus, for always wiping the slate clean so I can choose to look forward and live a life that honors you. Amen.

Daily Gratitude:

_____

_____

_____

_____

_____

_____

Reflections:

_____

_____

_____

_____

_____

_____

_____

_____

Day 70

Matthew 14:31-33

Jesus immediately reached out and grabbed him. "You have so little faith," Jesus said. "Why did you doubt me?" When they climbed back into the boat, the wind stopped. Then the disciples worshiped him. "You really are the Son of God!" they exclaimed.

Mindful Minute

When we feel like we are suffering through a storm, Jesus is always there to grab us and show us how calm can be created when we have faith. It is when we start doubting His plans for us that the storm within us rages, the seeds of fear grip us, and the anxiety of life becomes ever more present. The longer we walk this path, the easier it gets. Each temptation is less rooted in its neural pathway. Each time we succeed, we develop a different way to cope with stress and anxiety. Look up, have faith, and know there is something better He has planned for us.

When confronted with a storm in your life, remember to apply the LIE acronym when tempted to engage in something that is not consistent with God's plan for you. LOOK at the story you are telling yourself and identify its false nature. INTERCEPT that thought with a vision of your future self, the one God created for you, and EXPLORE alternative activities until the until the thought passes.

Prayer

Father, why do I waste a moment doubting your promises are real? I see so much evidence and truth to this. Help me this day and every day to practice faith and persistence in continuing to run this race without doubts. In Jesus' name, Amen.

Daily Gratitude:

_____

_____

_____

_____

_____

_____

Reflections:

_____

_____

_____

_____

_____

_____

_____

_____

_____

Week 11: Days 71–77

Day 71

Genesis 6:22

So Noah did everything exactly as God had commanded him.

Mindful Minute

This verse is repeated almost verbatim in Genesis 7:5 after more instruction is given about the animals to be taken into the ark. The remarkable thing about this statement is that what Noah was doing was almost certainly considered ludicrous by any worldly standard, bar none. Building a massive vessel in the middle of dry land and loading it with animals? Crazy, right? Noah did everything God asked because he knew God did it out of love for him. He knew God had a plan for him in the future.

As we are learning in this series of Scriptures, God is asking us to stay on the path and have faith in the much better plan He has for us. While we may not know what His plan is today, we can be certain about it as we continue to walk the path and believe. It is not always easy to ignore what is manifesting around us or what is being said about us as we walk a different path than what looks "normal" to others. We know, however, that doing everything as He has commanded will yield fruit in our lives and in the lives of others.

Ask God today, "What do you want of me?" Many times, it might be just a small and simple thing, such as sending someone a text or calling someone for a check-in. When you ask this question, listen for the answer, and obey like Noah did.

Prayer

Thank you, Father, for this day. I want to do everything you ask, especially as it relates to this habit of mine that has distracted me from living as fully as you intended. I want to find who I really am and who you created me to be. Thank you for the wisdom and guidance in your Word. It is so simple, yet so effective. Tell me today what you want of me so I can obey. Thank you, Jesus. Amen.

Daily Gratitude:

_____

_____

_____

_____

_____

_____

Reflections:

_____

_____

_____

_____

_____

_____

_____

_____

_____

_____

Day 72

Genesis 28:15

What's more, I am with you, and I will protect you wherever you go. One day I will bring you back to this land. I will not leave you until I have finished giving you everything I have promised you.

Mindful Minute

In this verse, God is speaking to Jacob in a dream. Jacob was promised that his descendants would be as numerous as the dust of the earth and all the families of the earth would be blessed through his descendants. Jacob was a man of God and suffered many travesties during his life, including the rape of his daughter and the death of his first love (his wife) during childbirth. His firstborn son slept with one of his concubines and forfeited his own path to leadership of his clan.

Walking with God does not mean an avoidance of heartache, but it does mean God will never forsake us. God never withheld His love, despite Jacob's transgressions, and He will be there for you too. He is there with each one of us every step of the way, and His promises enable us to endure. He will never forsake us.

Prayer

I cannot be reminded enough, Father, as I walk through life's difficult moments, how life is hard. I always need to be reminded, "You got this." One foot in front of the other, one deep breath at a time, knowing you see the other side, and it is glorious. Thank you, Jesus, for your sacrifice on the cross and for the gift of forgiveness that comes when I simply ask. Amen.

Daily Gratitude:

_____

_____

_____

_____

_____

_____

Reflections:

_____

_____

_____

_____

_____

_____

_____

_____

_____

Day 73

Proverbs 3:5-7

Trust in the Lord with all your heart; do not depend on your own understanding. Seek his will in all you do, and he will show you which path to take. Don't be impressed with your own wisdom. Instead, fear the Lord and turn away from evil.

Mindful Minute

There is much to focus on in this verse. We have removed our toxic habit for enough days at this point to see the benefits in a big way. There might be more questions we have about how our lives will play out going forward. Removing a life-interfering behavior solves many problems, but not all of them. We live in a sinful world, and it circles around us. Unexpected and heartfelt situations still come at us in our daily lives.

The clarity provided by removing psychological slavery is a powerful one. We are now able to assess situations with more confidence. When we feel His presence through the Holy Spirit, we are better able to stand with conviction in what is right and wrong for us. We can draw boundaries without anger or dread because we know we are standing on solid ground, *His* solid ground.

While we do not know what the future holds, we can trust Him with all our heart, knowing He knows the end of the story for each one of us.

Prayer

Father, as I walk this path of change in habits, this verse makes more and more sense. Life is not easy. Challenges continue to arise. Questions still need to be answered. I must stay the course and trust you in all circumstances. Too often, I gave in to earthly temptations. Now I have new and ever-present evidence of how shunning the evil associated with this habit produces truth, light, peace, and ultimate joy. Thank you, Jesus, for your wisdom and your sacrifice. Amen.

Daily Gratitude:

_____

_____

_____

_____

_____

_____

Reflections:

_____

_____

_____

_____

_____

_____

_____

_____

_____

Day 74

Galatians 5:22-23

But the Holy Spirit produces this kind of fruit in our lives: love, joy, peace, patience, kindness, goodness, faithfulness, gentleness, and self-control. There is no law against these things!

Mindful Minute

As you get closer to the end of this initial journey, it is important to document and remember the qualities produced through this twelve-week devotional. By removing this habit from our lives during this relatively short period, it becomes much easier to love, much easier to find happiness in simplicity, to have much more patience with those we love at home or deal with at work, and much easier to be kind in situations that would have previously tested our patience.

The concept of self-control is introduced here as well. God has given us the ability to choose, and we are gaining more and more evidence of how choosing a path consistent with His will brings us these fruits of the Spirit. Faith, and therefore faithfulness, also becomes stronger as we spend our mornings in His Word.

Our enemy roams around, looking for opportune times to tempt us back into our old ways. Stay on the path and prepare. The results have been well worth it.

Prayer

Father, as I gain more wins associated with choosing a path of righteousness regarding this life-interfering behavior and habit, I experience the fruits of the Spirit more deeply and consistently. What is surprising to me in this list is the concept of self-control. I can now see that in your perfect love, I can choose to love you with all my heart. This too is a choice! When I choose to love and honor you, I see how I have been given the ability to make other choices with more confidence. Thank you, Jesus! Amen.

Daily Gratitude:

_____

_____

_____

_____

_____

_____

Reflections:

_____

_____

_____

_____

_____

_____

_____

_____

_____

Day 75

1 Thessalonians 5:6

So be on your guard, not asleep like the others. Stay alert and be clearheaded.

Mindful Minute

Other versions of this verse use the words "alert and sober" in place of clearheaded. Either way, the inference is the same. We must develop an awareness of the things in this world that can lead our focus away from our Heavenly Father. We do this by continuing to pray and stay in His Word daily because this is how He speaks to each one of us. This is how we develop wisdom and discernment to continue to choose a path that follows His will for us.

Yes, being clearheaded allows for the avoidance of a variety of otherwise unfruitful conversations and decisions in our lives. It is much easier to make choices aligned with God when clearheaded. The word "asleep" here according to the *Expository Dictionary of Bible Words* means "spiritually asleep" and is further defined as a condition of insensibility to divine things involving conformity to the world.

Our influence in this world for all that is good is seen very clearly in staying "clearheaded."

Prayer

As this old habit of mine has receded further in the rearview mirror, it becomes clearer how much I did "sleep through" life. I was not as aware of the needs of others. I was not as present as I could have been in all my relationships, whether family, friends, or co-workers. I am awake, Father, and I am loving the freedom of existing this way. Thank you, Jesus. Amen.

Daily Gratitude:

_____

_____

_____

_____

_____

Reflections:

_____

_____

_____

_____

_____

_____

_____

_____

Day 76

Psalm 16:11

You will show me the way of life, granting me the joy of your presence and the pleasures of living with you forever.

Mindful Minute

With approximately one more week remaining in this journey, you have the opportunity to assess how much the needle has moved for you as a result of being successful in removing a behavior that once controlled your life. Have these practices of gratitude, study of His word, and being in His presence brought you more joy? Godly peace and joy are produced despite circumstances. Continue to take the time to document the wins that have come with choosing to avoid a toxic habit and harmful behavior and compare them with the reasons you chose to walk this path for twelve weeks. While there may still be some lingering romanticism about your habit, consider the scale of pros and cons, and remember them when temptation arises.

In the scientific world, there is a theory called "mirror neurons" where humans mimic the behaviors of others in their presence. The concept is that negativity breeds negativity and positivity breeds positivity.

When we have joy in the Lord, others take notice and wonder, 'What's your secret?' That's the kind of joy we want others to be drawn to, so much so that they want to experience it for themselves.

Prayer

While in the midst of the sin that took the form of a bad habit, this verse represented just words to me, Father. I believed and had faith in this truth but was never able to experience it. The path of life now seems easier. I am filled with more joy than I have experienced in a long time. The future remains uncertain, but as I step into it, I view life as full of possibilities for you to use my gifts for your glory. Thank you, Jesus. Amen.

Daily Gratitude:

_____

_____

_____

_____

_____

_____

Reflections:

_____

_____

_____

_____

_____

_____

_____

_____

_____

Day 77

Hebrews 5:13-14

For someone who lives on milk is still an infant and doesn't know how to do what is right. Solid food is for those who are mature, who through training have the skill to recognize the difference between right and wrong.

Mindful Minute

The verses in Hebrews prior to these were admonishing those who had "forgotten" God's truths, comparing their knowledge to infants. This unique twelve-week journey has allowed you to gain godly wisdom because of your commitment in experiencing Him directly by meditating on His Word each day (a kind of training). This daily practice is "spiritual food" for the soul. Prior to experiencing His Word directly, we may have thought the Bible was filled with a bunch of rules that make life dull and boring. Now, however, we have been made aware it is because of His love for us and His desire for us to avoid unnecessary and self-inflicted heartache.

There is enough heartache in this world on its own without us having to add to it needlessly by entertaining a behavior that stole our identity, our integrity, and may have also negatively affected those we care about. Let us move forward understanding the results of our choices—whether in our relationship with God, with those we have a chance to witness to, or with the people we want a deeper connection with.

Prayer

As I continue to move forward in this journey, one step at a time and one day at a time, I recognize how my power of discernment of good and evil is stronger through constant practice. The more I develop a good habit to replace the bad one, the easier it is to see how many other forms of sin I have allowed into my life. Moving further and further away from this habit has allowed me to not only distinguish good from evil but also has made it easier for me to choose good over evil moving forward. Thank you, Jesus. Amen.

Daily Gratitude:

_____

_____

_____

_____

_____

_____

Reflections:

_____

_____

_____

_____

_____

_____

_____

_____

_____

Week 12: Days 78–84

Day 78

Hebrews 10:24-25

Let us think of ways to motivate one another to acts of love and good works. And let us not neglect our meeting together, as some people do, but encourage one another, especially now that the day of his return is drawing near.

Mindful Minute

Jesus will return one day, and Matthew 24 tells us no one knows the day or the hour, which is why we must live each day as if it might be the day Jesus returns. Our relinquishment of this habit has not been a curse; it has been a blessing. To the extent we can continue to live a life that is inspirational for others, this alone is worth the journey.

Many quietly suffer from the same pain of this psychological slavery, and you have been empowered through the Holy Spirit to love and motivate them simply by showing there is another way to live. Meeting together refers to church gatherings or active fellowship with other believers.

If you are not actively meeting with other believers, consider choosing a church or other gathering of faith that feels like home to you. There you will be able to share and encourage others through your own experiences.

Prayer

Father, so many times we look outward for scientific validation of our faith, yet time and again your Word has shown us how it is perfect instruction for teaching and succeeding. Meeting in groups, discussing the truth of our struggles, spurring one another on to do good, and loving each other unconditionally remain powerful ways to encourage good habits and confidence. It is only when we bring the darkness into the light and find love and acceptance that we can see our full potential. Thank you, Jesus. Amen.

Daily Gratitude:

_____

_____

_____

_____

_____

_____

Reflections:

_____

_____

_____

_____

_____

_____

_____

_____

_____

Day 79

1 Thessalonians 5:11

So encourage each other and build each other up, just as you are already doing.

Mindful Minute

There is so much negativity and intolerance in the world today. A quick glance at the news or an election ad reveals the gut-wrenching tactics people use to get our attention. Sadly, those tactics often work.

But encouragement works too. And it brings life.

According to a 2014 *Forbes* article by success coach Cathy Caprino, people who positively impact the world do more than get results. They uplift others as they go. Their energy inspires growth. They are generous with help and genuinely want others to succeed.

As you reflect on your journey today, think about how your presence might encourage someone else. You do not need to change the entire world. You can start by inspiring just one person. That is how true impact begins.

God has a plan for you. Keep walking this path with curiosity, looking for ways your God-given gifts can bring light to the people around you. Who might you encourage today?

Prayer

Thank you for your wisdom this day, Father. As I walk through this journey, I recognize the absolute power to lift others up that has been given to each one of us. It is only in you, with gratitude and thanksgiving and hope, that I can look in the eyes of another and pass on inspiration and hope to them. Thank you, Jesus. Amen.

Daily Gratitude:

_____

_____

_____

_____

_____

_____

Reflections:

_____

_____

_____

_____

_____

_____

_____

_____

_____

Day 80

2 Timothy 1:7

For God has not given us a spirit of fear and timidity, but of power, love, and self-discipline.

Mindful Minute

Scripture tells us the hairs on our head are numbered, and each one of us was given a unique spiritual gift. In Him, we can be fearless about who we were created to be, and curious about the purpose He has planned for us. We continue to recognize how God gave us the ability to choose and the "power" to love and have self-discipline. Through His guidance and our perseverance, we do not need to apologize for who we are, and we should be bold and confident with our gifts.

What is stopping you from experiencing this power? Is it a wound caused by the sin of others or by your own choices? Remember, we are forgiven when we go to the cross with a repentant heart. It is worth repeating that forgiveness is the process of wiping the slate clean. Accepting His forgiveness means that we are free to look forward to something new and leave the past in the past. This doesn't mean we have amnesia about the past, but it does mean we have been freed of the chains that tied us down to it.

The Lord's Prayer also asks us to forgive others as we have been forgiven. These two acts provide us with true freedom to move forward without apology and boldly proclaim our faith through love and self-discipline.

Prayer

Father, I see that in receiving your unconditional love and forgiveness, I have been successful in choosing this path to leave behind a habit that did not serve me. In doing so, my self-confidence continues to increase. Please bless me this day to use this newfound confidence to reflect your light to others. Thank you, Jesus. Amen.

Daily Gratitude:

_____

_____

_____

_____

_____

_____

Reflections:

_____

_____

_____

_____

_____

_____

_____

_____

_____

Day 81

Acts 9:18

Instantly something like scales fell from Saul's eyes, and he regained his sight. Then he got up and was baptized.

Mindful Minute

Saul went from killing followers of Jesus to having the scales fall off his eyes to see the world through the eyes of our Lord. As a result, Saul was baptized and renamed Paul. Paul is traditionally credited with writing at least half the books of the New Testament. When we spend time with God, our sight is restored, and His Word comes alive to us in a way that was previously not possible. Paul went from being a passionate persecutor of Christians to a passionate apostle for Christ. He used his past as a story of testimony and hope to illustrate how things can and will change when we believe.

You have a story as well that can be used to inspire others. Do not let the sins of the past (whether yours or those of others) define or interfere with who God created you to be. Reflect on how God has spoken to you through this walk and continue to ask for guidance in your direction for the future.

Take advantage of the newfound patience and peace gained by resting in Him and resisting temptation. Confidently try new things, create new relationships, improve the ones that exist today, and continue testing what is "good."

Prayer

Thank you, Father, for this time with you each morning. The more time I spend with you, the more I feel at peace because of your love and guidance. Taking away this sinful habit has allowed me to remove the scales from my own eyes in so many areas of my life. I want to continue this journey with you so I can walk with my eyes fully open. Thank you, Jesus, for your loving sacrifice so I can see more clearly. Amen.

Daily Gratitude:

_____

_____

_____

_____

_____

_____

Reflections:

_____

_____

_____

_____

_____

_____

_____

_____

Day 82

Colossians 3:15

And let the peace that comes from Christ rule in your hearts. For as members of one body you are called to live in peace. And always be thankful.

Mindful Minute

The biblical word for peace in Greek is *eirene* (i-ray'-nay). According to *Strong's Concordance*, it means one, peace, quietness, and rest. It originates from the word *eiro*, which means to join or tie together into a whole. The peace that comes from Christ means a state of being whole and complete, lacking nothing.

As we focus more on the last few days of our journey, we can take time to reflect on how much more peace has been embedded into our lives as we put our habit in the rearview mirror and look forward. This does not mean our lives are suddenly perfect or without disruption. Many may still be dealing with personal unresolved conflicts. The peace that comes from Christ is different, and Philippians 4:6-7 explains it well, confirming how our practice of daily gratitude helps us to achieve it:

> Don't worry about anything. Instead, pray about everything. Tell God what you need and thank him for all he has done. Then you will experience God's peace, which exceeds anything we can understand. His peace will guard your hearts and minds as you live in Christ Jesus.

Prayer

Yes, Father, turmoil swirls around me daily, but practicing and living according to your loving instruction allows me to have the peace in my heart you have promised. The further away the bad habit is, the more peace I experience in you. Thank you, Jesus, for paying the price for my sin. I could not imagine life without you. Amen.

Daily Gratitude:

_____

_____

_____

_____

_____

_____

Reflections:

_____

_____

_____

_____

_____

_____

_____

_____

_____

Day 83

Matthew 6:34

So don't worry about tomorrow, for tomorrow will bring its own worries. Today's trouble is enough for today.

Mindful Minute

As we close in on the conclusion of this twelve-week journey, it is time to consider how we move forward with freedom from the behavior that used to control our lives. After all, wasn't this meant to be just a short-term test? At the beginning of this journey, we agreed to meditate on God's Word and experience firsthand the strength, guidance, and love that is bestowed upon us as we meditate on it. We put aside this habit and have witnessed firsthand the benefits of removing something that had such a negative stronghold on our lives.

It is now time to document your observations about the benefits of removing this habit that produced sin in your life so when you're tempted, you can "play the movie through to the end." Our best defense moving forward is to focus on today. The Lord's Prayer is simple and all-encompassing, including the phrase "Give us *this day* our daily bread." While we can plan for tomorrow and think about the future, worrying about it adds nothing to our experience of the present moment. As far as neurological habits go, the more we practice today, the better tomorrow gets. Every day that is a win produces easier days in the future.

Focus on getting through today and each day moving forward by living in the moment and appreciating everything around you, because everything good comes from God.

Prayer

Father, there are so many reasons to be anxious in this world. I choose gratitude and thankfulness this day over worry. True peace is only possible when I trust you for the results. My daily practices in your loving instruction have produced a peace I have not experienced before. I no longer need to live in guilt, shame, and anxiety about my actions related to this habit. Thank you, Jesus, for your sacrifice and allowing me to live in peace, knowing I have been forgiven. Amen.

Daily Gratitude:

_____

_____

_____

_____

_____

_____

Reflections:

_____

_____

_____

_____

_____

_____

_____

_____

_____

Day 84

3 John 1:2

Dear friend, I hope all is well with you and that you are as healthy in body as you are strong in spirit.

Mindful Minute

Isn't a healthy body and spirit something all of us want? This is something we should not take for granted, as a child might. We must continue to practice and ingrain good habits in our minds and bodies so they become second nature and create new neural pathways. How has your health and spirit fared during this journey?

Continue to spend time with God as He guides you in your path. Continue to assess and document your progress spiritually, psychologically, and physically to understand the impact of spending this time with Him in His Word. Are you willing to make choices that would send you back to the way things were? The stress that was created in us by the psychological slavery of this habit negatively affected our overall health and well-being.

We are running this race called life, and we will continue to learn and grow in all aspects if we choose to do so. The channels of "this world" will remain deceptive in communications that sell us sex, shiny objects, and riches, but as we connect more with Him, we will develop the confidence and practices necessary for success in finding the self we were created to be.

Prayer

Thank you for this day, Father, as I begin to recognize the positive changes from setting aside this habit. It affected not only my physical, spiritual, and emotional well-being, but also impacted my relationships and sense of joy. I see now how it added unnecessary stress, distraction, and discouragement to my life. Yes, Father, caring for my health truly does go well with my soul. Thank you, Jesus. Amen.

Daily Gratitude:

_____

_____

_____

_____

_____

Reflections:

_____

_____

_____

_____

_____

_____

_____

_____

Epilogue

*W*OW! You did it. You made it through a grueling twelve weeks, investing significantly in *you*! Initially it was tough. But if you are like most, even though you experienced some ups and downs, you persevered and now have significantly more control over your life-interfering habit.

Let's use a simple example to explain what's happened inside your spirit, mind, and body.

Let's say you look in the mirror and examine your physique. Then you drop to the floor and do one solid pushup. You stand up, glance at the mirror again, and see the same worn-out body staring back at you. No visible change. But something *was* happening. Even though you couldn't see it, small but important shifts were taking place beneath the surface. Your muscles, tendons, ligaments, and bones were all engaged and responding.

That one pushup made it easier to do another the next day. By day three, you could do a few more. Then five. A week later, you were doing ten. A couple of weeks in, fifteen. By the end of the month, you were doing twenty-five in a row. You look in the mirror again and this time—wow—you *see* the change. But remember, the real transformation began before it was visible. It started with consistency, commitment, and the belief that what you were doing mattered, even if no one could see it yet.

Now let's be clear, you just experienced this same process. But not your shoulders, chest, and triceps. Something not only better, but way more powerful. If you were grinding your daily pushups, we call devotionals, for twelve weeks, your brain circuits, thinking mind, and inner spirit have undergone a radical macroscopic transformation! Just like when we physically grow—others notice your growth but you don't—some of you might not have noticed your amazing spirit, mind, and body growth, and need to better tune your radar to appreciate the changes.

News Flash: Your new circuits are becoming your well-worn default settings, and the old brain ruts are starting to fill in with debris and are less easily accessed. PsychoSpiritual slavery to your life-interfering behavior is cast aside and traded for true freedom through the power, connection, and light of the Holy Spirit.

Let's fine-tune your radar to notice your macroscopic changes. Review your notes and reflections throughout the twelve-week process as you answer the following questions:

- Do you sleep better?
- Do you have less anxiety and stress?
- Overall, is your mood better?
- Are you calmer?
- Do you have better control over your emotions?
- Do you feel more connected to God?
- Have you managed to forgive yourself and others?
- Have you learned more about the B.I.B.L.E. (Best Instruction Book for Living Everyday)?
- Are you more empowered to continue the healing plan God's designed for you and you for?
- Are your relationships better?
- Has your performance at work and/or in the home improved?
- Do you see a better path for yourself?
- Do you notice a spiritual awakening/reawakening happening inside you?
- Do you have more confidence in yourself?
- Do you have more time for self-care?
- Are you making less excuses for your decisions/behaviors?
- Compared to 12 weeks ago, do you trust yourself more to make a plan and stick to it?
- Compared to 12 weeks ago, do you think you have more mind skills?
- Compared to 12 weeks ago, do you feel more valued?
- Compared to 12 weeks ago, do you see some purpose becoming clearer?
- What other macroscopic changes do you notice?
- What other macroscopic changes have others noticed?

This task reflecting and highlighting your transformational changes needs to be completed because it's DECISION TIME! Time for you to make a choice of how you're going to move forward. Three paths exist, which will you take?

1. Especially if the past twelve weeks have been a significant struggle, you might think moving past your life-interfering behavior has been hard, too much work, painful, with lots of grieving and loss. You fantasize about the distraction, relief, escape, or buzz when you engage your old habit. Sadly, we often have amnesia for all the pain, hurt, loss, struggle, effort, and payments (physical, psychological, relational, emotional, spiritual, financial, and maybe even legal) we made. Not to mention the hurt we caused others. Reality and the BIBLE clearly teach this core truth, no pain-free option for growth exists. Sure the new way is painful initially, but pain gives way to lots of joy as we stay the course. The old way is painful too, especially in the beginning, but unlike the new path, it only gets more painful the longer you stay on it. The choice should be clear. Keep walking the new path.

2. On the flip side, if the last twelve weeks have been successful, minimal relapses, and fairly "easy," you might be tempted to walk down the complacency and over-confidence path. Often romanticizing about or positively spinning behaviors that were actually a source of toxicity in your life. Many will end up entertaining a false and dangerous narrative about how they can now test the waters in a more "controlled" manner. Your body is back in balance, and your confidence is high, but do not be deceived. The old circuits and operating system embedded in your neurological pathways have been quieted but can easily be woken up and lead to a path of destruction. You will continue to run into situations that surprise you in terms of how powerful the temptation can be, and there will be situational temptations that are also extremely enticing.

3. Whether the past twelve weeks were easy or hard, you know you want true peace, joy, and freedom. What is God calling you to do now? You don't know yet? Don't worry, just trust that He does have a plan! Continue to walk the straight and healthy path you're now walking! Macroscopic changes are happening already, and you will be amazed what new changes each 3-month season brings. But beware, the enemy will offer many exit ramps off this path that advertise shortcuts to peace, freedom, joy, fulfillment. He only has one purpose and that is to "steal, kill and destroy" (John 10:10 ESV). Sadly, all paths he offers lead to destruction. Only your Creator knows how your mind performs the best, so resist the impostor's shortcuts and stay the course on your Creator's path to your abundant and transformed life.

If you feel stuck or sense that you need more help, contact Dr. Karl at Honey Lake Clinic to explore treatment options by visiting www.honeylake.clinic or calling 215-630-8846.

by His grace,
Dr. Karl and Rose Ann Forte

If This Book Helped You…

We hope Transformed by His Promises has been a meaningful step on your journey toward a Spirit-filled life beyond life-interfering behaviors. If the guidance and reflections in these pages have inspired or empowered you, would you consider sharing your experience?

Here's how you can help:

1. **Leave a Review**
   Putting a review on the platform where you purchased this book is a great way to help others discover it.

2. **Spread the Word**
   Tell a friend, family member, or someone in your community about this book.

About The Authors

Karl Benzio, M.D., is a uniquely gifted psychiatrist and devoted follower of Christ who has spent 35+ years integrating psychiatric science and the Bible to transform lives. With foundational training in biomedical engineering and psychiatry, Dr. Karl's led thousands to healing by teaching how Godly decision-making renews and rewires the brain—a core tenet of his Practical NeuroTheology and SPEARS decision-making model. As Co-Founder of Honey Lake Clinic and Medical Director for the American Association of Christian Counselors, he consults internationally, testifies before policy bodies, and is a frequent media guest speaking widely on Christian psychiatry and behavioral neuroscience. A former addict himself, Dr. Karl offers credibility and compassion, helping people overcome anxiety, depression, addiction, poor decision-making, and destructive habits. Married since 1991, a father of three, and a passionate ice cream and pickleball enthusiast, he equips readers to couple God's "instruction manual" with practical brain-based strategies for lasting peace, joy, and freedom (drkarlbenzio.com).

Rose Ann Forte is an international, award-winning, bestselling author, speaker, and creator of the Choose Freedom Program, a biblically based and neuroscience-informed path to help individuals overcome alcohol and other life-interfering behaviors. After personally experiencing transformation through God's renewing truth, she felt called to share her journey and the tools that led to her freedom. She first introduced her faith-based methodology in *The Plans He Has for Me Daily Devotional*, followed by *Prepare to Quit*, a practical guide for those exploring their relationship with alcohol. In *Transformed by His Promises*, Rose Ann partners with psychiatrist Karl Benzio, M.D. to expand her devotional model to all life-interfering behaviors, combining biblical promises with brain science to equip readers for lasting change. Rose Ann is passionate about equipping coaches, counselors, and faith-based organizations with tools that restore hope and transform lives. She also hosts the podcast *Say Goodbye and Imagine!* and lives in Phoenix, Arizona.

www.ingramcontent.com/pod-product-compliance
Lightning Source LLC
Chambersburg PA
CBHW080818120626
46556CB00010B/3329